Snapshots

Snapshots

STEVEN FORREST

iUniverse, Inc.
Bloomington

Snapshots

iUniverse books may be ordered through booksellers or by contacting:

iUniverse
1663 Liberty Drive
Bloomington, IN 47403
www.iuniverse.com
1-800-Authors (1-800-288-4677)

ISBN: 978-1-4620-3409-3 (sc)
ISBN: 978-1-4620-3410-9 (dj)
ISBN: 978-1-4620-3411-6 (ebk)

Printed in the United States of America

iUniverse rev. date: 07/19/2011

Forward . . .

In February 2006, I was involved in an accident that by all accounts should have ended my life. Through incredible coincidence and personal circumstance, somehow I survived—I don't really understand why, I just did. The easiest way to explain it is to say I was rejected by death. The impetus for this journey comes from my daughter, Alicia, who composed a very sincere, heartfelt and touching essay about my accident for her English class assignment at the tender age of 11 years. A portion of that essay is included here. Although her essay is not entirely accurate, the depth of her emotion and expression will capture yours. It certainly did mine.

Building Bones
By: Alicia Forrest

Would you believe that someone that you would give the world for could die while you were away at school? I didn't until it happened to me. Because of this, I believe I can make the world a better place by helping others hold onto their loved ones for just a bit longer. I can do this by becoming an orthopedic surgeon. Why an orthopedic surgeon, you might ask? Well, here is my story.

A cool breeze blew orange and red leaves across the front yard of a white and green, conservative house in Washington. Fall, as you know, is when trees lose their summer colors and drop their autumn finery, for bare-bone branches of white, cold, winter silk. During this season, the winds tend to pick up in Washington, quite alarmingly, and blow the weaker trees over.

During one of these gusts of wind, a weak maple tree fell over on my dad and step-mom's house. This caused my dad great alarm and reason to think about how many trees he wanted around his house. My dad started thinking about cutting down the weak Maple saplings. Our house was not damaged, but soon, my dad thought, if the trees kept on falling, it would be.

One morning, my dad decided that he was going to leave his cozy Washington abode and do something about the trees. He thought he would go cut them down and, perhaps, even make a profit off of them, selling them as lumber. Slowly, he put on his heavy winter jacket, and pulled on his leather, lace-up boots. He wrapped a navy blue scarf around his neck and pulled on his sturdiest Levi Strauss's. He wandered into the kitchen and put a piece of Potato bread in the toaster and filled a mug up with coffee. Drinking his coffee, he waited for his toast to pop up.

When his toast was done, he put on butter and jam, and munched it up as he walked out the door. As he walked out the door, Carol, my step-mom yelled cheerily, "Be careful Steve. Don't get too cold!" My dad nodded his head as he walked to the garage and picked up his chain-saw. Our sweet dog, Shade, loyally followed my dad. Shade, a big black Lab, would go anywhere with my dad. Lumbering down the hill, my dad thought about the football scores and what he might eat for lunch. When he got to the bottom of the hill, he set down his mug of coffee and got down to business.

Shade, eagerly watching, found a good spot to lie down and rested his head on his huge, black paws. My dad yanked the cord on the chainsaw and warmed it up. Placing the chainsaw "just so" on the tree trunk for the correct angle, he began cutting the tree down. When my dad was about 7/8ths of the way through the tree, he walked to the other side of the cut, pushed, and yelled, "Timber!" The tree creaked in protest and then crashed down to the ground. My dad thought, "Piece of cake. Only a couple more to go." The next tree was much bigger; a good three feet taller. My dad was so "pumped up" from the other tree that he did not bother taking all the safety precautions he had before. He angled the blade on the side of the tree and began cutting.

Suddenly, the tree trunk snapped and the tree fell down on my father. Luckily, my two wonderful neighbors were walking down the hill through the forest and heard Shade barking and howling. They ran to see what was wrong and found, to their horror, my dad unconscious, underneath a huge maple tree, with Shade at his side, frantically barking. Meem, an ER nurse, called 911. A Portland hospital helicopter rushed to my dad's rescue. The tree had crushed my dad's leg and some ribs.

If it weren't for Shade barking, my dad would have died. Meem also saved my dad's life by calling 911 and giving him First Aid. As the helicopter whirled overhead, Carol ran down the hill, tears streaming from her eyes. "Steve! Steve! Where is he? What happened?" The paramedics cut the tree into pieces and lifted the tree off my dad's broken body. The emergency crew carefully lifted my dad onto a gurney, and rushed him off to the hospital, miles away. Carol watched in tears as the helicopter lifted off and sped away.

At the hospital, surgeons in their scrubs and sterile booties, put on masks and gloves, preparing for surgery. The helicopter landed on the roof of the hospital in Portland. The paramedics rushed my dad into the theatre for life-saving care. When Carol arrived at the hospital, the doctor came out of the surgery room and told her, "This isn't looking good. We do not know if Steve will survive the night. Even if he does, he may lose his leg. We will do our best. I am so sorry."

That night, I was doing my homework in our old recliner when the phone rang. I assumed it was just a regular old telemarketer, because my mom was silent for the first few seconds. Then my mom came in the room, and solemnly said, "Your dad has just had a major accident. We do not know if he will live the night. Just keep him in your prayers." My mom hugged me and walked down the hall silently, pondering what to say to me if my dad passed away. I just sat in the recliner, stunned. I felt as if my spine had disappeared. I slumped down into the chair and couldn't breathe. My mouth dropped open. In shock, I just stared in a daze at the floor. What did she say? How could he have had an accident? I talked to him yesterday! I can't believe this. This can't be real . . . or can it?

That year my grades went down and I almost did not make it into 7th grade honors classes. My future seemed bleak. I did not know what to do with my life. The day after the horrible news, my mom told me my dad would live but it would be a very long recovery. He probably would walk with a limp, if he could ever walk again. But that still did not help the way I felt about my life.

Thankfully, a few months later, I got the best Christmas gift of all: my dad's life. I went up to Portland and visited him in the hospital. He was in the hospital for three months. He couldn't even talk or eat the first week in the hospital. My dad always tells me that when I first saw him in the hospital, I stood over him, grim faced, like I was an angel guarding him. I did not say a word. I just stood there. And though many people do not know this, while I was standing there, a tear rolled down my cheek and landed on the hospital blanket covering my dad's injured leg. Just one tear. I did not break into tears or sob; I just silently cried all my misery into one tear; one tear of healing, which I gave to my dad . . .

Each time I read her words, which has been often, I take a deep breath and sigh as I am overwhelmed by emotion and the love of a young girl. Near the end of my story I will explain what actually happened that day and the rationale for the reason I am here to write this story. Purely a miracle . . .

Snowbird 1980

for my daughter, Alicia, and my son, Chris . . .

Alicia

Chris

. . . **Snapshots**

"You might wake up some morning,
To the sound of something moving past your window in the wind.
And if you're quick enough to rise,
You'll catch the fleeting glimpse of someone's fading shadow . . .

. . . Bob Lind

Writing my life's adventures for you both will be a daunting and oftentimes emotionally piercing endeavor for the simple reason that truth is difficult to examine when your view of it is understandably slanted. Sprinkled throughout are humorous moments of playful tenderness along with a deep longing for acceptance which are common place in everyone's life. Tender, emotional tears flowed from me as I reminisced and wrote, and emotions will rise in you when you read the untold secrets of my distant and uneasy past life, but how many children have the opportunity to "see" their parent exposed as just an ordinary person. On the other hand, there are many joyous moments, too, so don't take this as gloomy. It really isn't that way at all. Objectively, you will discover your father was just a man,

ix

sometimes not a very good one and sometimes a really terrific guy who searched most of his life (unknown to everyone) to find a lost love. He was just an ordinary man on an extraordinary quest who cared deeply for his children while struggling with personal relationships; one who made more than his share of mistakes and yet a man who gave freely of himself for others, and that's the best part. There is nothing spectacular in this account, except honesty. I will reveal events in my life that have been kept in the deepest part of my memory for decades; their revelation will be alarming and may cause you wonderment, and yet I hope sincerely you two can learn from them as I will do my best to lay out many of the trappings of life. These are some of the snapshots of my life, not all of them, just a collection of tender moments that have risen to my conscience in my search for thought and truth. I know all too well that you will both trip, stumble and fall. That's the easy part. The challenging part that will build your strength of character will be how well you manage adversity once it has cast its dark and ever-gripping shadow on you.

Venture out and explore the world with open eyes and feel what life has to offer. Life is a truly wonderful gift; don't waste it by endlessly seeking what can't be sought, although you probably will. The old saying about he who dies with the most toys wins is true, but that is a very lonely existence. Everything in life is temporary, although most people won't admit that. No one owes you anything and your greatest happiness in life will come from self-fulfillment of personal goals and the ceaseless giving of yourself to others (sharing). Sharing is the most meaningful and easily the most important thing you will ever do. So to both of my precious children I say, "Dance through life with a smile, you'll be better for it."

> "Do not follow where the path may lead. Go instead where there is no path and leave a trail."
> . . . Ralph Waldo Emerson

Throughout "Snapshots" I will offer you what I perceive to be some of life's truths, so take them with a grain of salt. What I mean is that the older I get, the wiser I become, and the less I know. So here is my first offering: no one can make you happy, only you can do that, and no one can cause you pain and unhappiness unless you give them permission.

Live your life for yourself and the ones you love and enjoy every "moment" of it. As much as you possibly can, fill your life with moments of beauty and joy and spirituality. Everyone on this planet is born, lives and dies alone. How you journey through life will depend on how well you cope, how well you speak, and mostly how well others perceive the real person in you and respond in kind. The one thing in life you can never run from is truth; it is the safest haven. Your happiness will be found from within and from your interaction with the others in your life space.

I wish you both the very best in life. As you read my story, remember it's your dad's life and no one else's so keep what is worth keeping and with a breath of kindness, blow the rest away. Each of you is an artist with your own canvass and paints. You paint paradise, and when you do, paint it softly and without regret . . .

Love,
Dad

Chapter 1: The beginning . . .

Often while drifting away in thought I have pictured myself telling you two how I grew up by painting vivid descriptions of my past. I say this because, admittedly, I am a dreamer and a painter. Is it important that I accomplish this task? Only to me. Because we have spent so many years apart, I hope you enjoy these expressions of your father's trip through life, and yet I realize that you both will be amazed at the truths revealed. Since I know you both love music, I'll sprinkle the names of songs throughout my story to give you a glimpse of the music I grew up with and the songs that captured my emotions. At times I will place the lyrics from certain songs in my story to expose a glimpse of my true feelings and the accompanying emotions that have painted my memories. Music has a way of transcending words and bringing emotion into your thoughts, at least it does for me. I don't believe I am much different from anyone else in that regard, but, heck, what do I know. There will be laughs and tears, so buckle up and enjoy the ride. Let's get started . . .

I was born March 13, 1945, on a Tuesday evening near the end of a blustery winter. My birth certificate states that I was born in Paris, Texas, and that I was the first child of Forrest Clayton Steven and Mary Grace Anderson. My name at birth was given as Forrest Clayton Steven, Jr. Not until I was a teenager did my mom tell me the real story of my birth.

My mom's family was very much gypsy-like and traveled continually from Louisiana to Texas to California to Oregon and back. They were always on the move as my grandfather, Charles (everyone called him Charlie), created billboards along Route 66 and U.S. 101. I know nothing of my dad's family.

Route 66, also known as U.S. Route 66, The Main Street of America, The Mother Road and the Will Rogers Highway, was a highway in the old U.S. Highway system. One of the original federal routes, Route 66 was established on November 11, 1926, though signs did not go up until the following year. It originally ran from Chicago, Illinois, through Missouri, Kansas, Oklahoma, Texas, New Mexico, Arizona, and California, before ending at Los Angeles for a total of 2,448 miles.

U.S. 101 is the most historic highway in California. It follows the route the Spanish explorer Juan Gaspar de Portola followed in 1769, which later became El Camino Real (the King's Highway). This historic road connected the 21 missions of California and served as the main north/south road in California until the 1920s. North of San Francisco it is known as the "Redwood Highway," which is considered by many to be the most scenic road in the U.S.

My grandparents were Charles and Helen Anderson. When I was young, my mom told me her parents immigrated from France and came to this country after World War I, settling in Louisiana where they could speak their native French. True to their heritage, they had a very large family. I only vaguely remember my grandfather as he passed away when I was about 5 years old. My grandmother, on the other hand, was quite a character. She didn't speak English very well which made her an unwitting comic. She spoke in broken English with French mixed in and the conversations with her were always entertaining, as they were with her brother, Ben (Benjamin).

My Uncle Ben (actually my mom's uncle—I just called him Uncle Ben) spoke better English than my grandmother probably because he spoke in slow motion. Seems like everything he did was in slow motion. He was 6'5" tall and had the sweetest disposition a man could want. Ben was a chef in New Orleans and I was continually reminded by my aunts that he was one of the best. Ben taught me how to make French toast so sweet that syrup was not necessary. The secret, Ben explained, was not to be in a hurry. "Be quick, but never in a hurry. Hurry," Ben said, "causes friction. Friction causes fire, and fire destroys." Imagine him saying that. My grandparents had 9 children: Charles, Robert, James, John, Helen,

Mary (mom), Hilda, Louise and . . . and . . . (it will come to me). It finally did: Albert.

Most of my aunts and uncles were born in Louisiana; some were born in Texas. My mom was born on a hot, humid August afternoon in the small town of Payne, just outside of Baton Rouge, the capitol city of Louisiana, in 1924. She was a petite southern girl, very attractive, who spoke French and English. At 5'2" and 105 pounds, she was not an imposing figure, but she commanded respect from her children. She had jet-black hair and piercing brown eyes. She was a pretty woman. All who knew her called her Gracie. Her children just called her Mama.

Mom was gregarious and light on her feet. She talked to her children (and jokingly to herself) all the time on almost any subject that came to her mind. She was affable by nature and loved music. Having been raised as a child in Louisiana, she was truly fond of country music, although she enjoyed swing and pop as well. On most days I can remember her singing to herself as she filled the house with warmth while doing chores; her voice was crystal clear even though she would say she could not sing as well as her sisters. Perhaps not, but we didn't care. Mom made us feel special and loved. She would fill our heads with picturesque, expressive visions of life and of things that could be. She was a dreamer and she passed that trait on to me. Even though we were not a prosperous family, she was a very strict parent and yet so very proud of all of us. I remember her calling me her "precious, delicate child" during card games with my aunts. I was anything but that.

Mom

3

One lazy summer afternoon in 1959, just before I started high school in Baldwin Park, she told me the story of my birth and the early years that I could not remember. She explained I was born in a small, beautiful parish in the French Quarter of New Orleans, Louisiana—not in Texas. Also, I was not born in a hospital. Rather, I was born in a small, cozy bed at home with my mom's sisters acting as nurses. I have a cousin named Paul Gardner who was born in the same bed exactly two months earlier. Paul and I would be close for years, until he went into the Army and we lost contact.

Because our families were continually on the move, I didn't have a birth certificate, neither did Paul. With tender, loving words my mom explained further that there was a war going on in Europe and in the Pacific and that spending money to have a child born in a hospital when you had no roots to call home was not an important issue in those days, especially when families stretched finances as far as could be done. Later, when we moved to northeast Texas in the spring, both my mom and her sister, Helen (Paul's mom), obtained birth certificates for us in the town of Paris, Texas. Shortly thereafter, the families moved again, to California in the summer of 1945. Paul and I were each other's best friend growing up, that is, when we saw each other. There was always a smile on our faces when we greeted one another. His family, however, continued their nomadic existence and our visits together became infrequent. I missed him when he was not around and I still do at times.

The war years were difficult on mom. When I was born my dad was in the Army, overseas in Europe. He entered the military in 1944 and left a pregnant wife at home to fight Hitler in Europe. He was fighting in Germany during World War II as a machine-gunner attached to General George Patton's regiment. He was born in February, 1925, in Chicago, Illinois. He was 5'9" tall and weighed about 160. He had hazel eyes and a very muscular build. In his younger days, he was quite a handsome man. His father (my grandfather) was named Clarence, but I know little about him, except that he worked for Union Pacific Railroad. Only once did I meet him and the experience left me feeling uneasy. I never met my grandmother (dad's mom) and I don't even know her name. That's sad. When I was young, perhaps 8 or 9 years old, I remember seeing pictures of a department store in Illinois called "Steven's." Other than that, I have no recollection of my dad's family.

After the war, my dad returned to the states where he was discharged from the Army, and reunited with my mother in Los Angeles in early 1946. Once again we pulled up roots and headed north to the city of Turlock. I have no clear memories of that period, but I do remember when my sister came home. She cried all the time and I didn't like it much.

It was in the middle of the spring of 1947 when my little sister, Ginger, was born on May 10, 1947, in Turlock, California, a small community just west of Stockton. She was christened Mary Virginia Steven, but we just called her Ginger. She had light brown hair and hazel eyes, like her dad's. She was a happy child and was always beaming a smile. Like most young girls, she enjoyed "dress-up" and playing "make believe." I have memories of her trudging around the house in her mom's cloths and shoes. The thing I remember most about my little sister is that we argued a lot, just like siblings do everywhere. I think I won most of the arguments, but the spankings I received from my mom when Ginger told on me tell a far different story. You see, Ginger was mom's favorite and really could do no wrong, or so it seemed. I do remember her smile, though. It was enchanting. In the evenings, mom would sing a catchy Perry Como tune to Ginger and rock her cradle. (Chi-Baba Chi-Baba—Perry Como)

Ginger (on right)

Shortly after Ginger was born, our family was on the move back to Southern California where my mom was to take a stand that would alter all our lives for the better. She told my dad that she wanted "roots" and would no longer move aimlessly around the country. She was the first in her family to do so. Seems there were lots of "firsts" in our family. A couple years later, mom's sister, Louise, would do the same, followed by her brothers Bobby and Johnny. The rest of her siblings continued their nomadic, gypsy existence and would be here today and gone tomorrow, but would always reunite for a family get together. It may seem hard to believe, but at my last recollection, I had 72 first cousins on my mother's side of the family. The largest clan belonged to Helen who had 10 children.

My earliest childhood memories drift back to the late 1940s when we lived on Temple Street in downtown Los Angeles. I am 3 or 4 years old and I am sitting on a tricycle talking to a little girl. Who she is is unimportant. I am smiling and showing off my "professor" glasses.

My dad called me "the professor" because of the dark-rimmed glasses I wore as a child. I was 18 months old when I had surgery on my right eye. At birth, it was not aligned properly and I had no functionality with it. I don't remember that part; my mom told me when I was a little older. I wore glasses until I was nearly 18 years old and probably should have continued, but vanity got in the way. Besides, my eyesight would never improve as I was told by several optometrists over the years that my left eye was so dominant that the right eye would only function if the left eye was injured. Left with that situation, I chose not to continue wearing glasses.

In early 1950 or 1951 we moved into a new house in Norwalk, California; the price was $7,000 as I recall. I remember the address of the first house my parents bought: 11523 E. Brimley Street, Norwalk, California. In early 1953, mom bought a new 1953 Buick (two-toned, yellow with black accents). My dad had another car that he drove to work, a Ford wagon. I don't know the year or model. I do remember the house, though. It was a small, white two bedroom house with a brown roof. There was a covered barbeque pit in the back that my dad built and lots of flowers that mom planted. While helping my dad one day I dropped a 4x4 and smashed my left big toe. That was a very painful incident that is etched in my mind.

Leading from the barbeque pit was a long, narrow cement walk-way to the back door of the house. The yard was green and neatly kept. In February 1953 a third child was born to our family: Kim Martin Russell Steven.

He looked, and still does, exactly like his dad. Kim was a quiet child, yet he always, always found ways to get into trouble. It was a trait that left a bleakly foreboding future for him. (Rag Mop—The Ames Brothers)

Living on Brimley Street meant adventure and accidents. We had friendly neighbors who had twin girls named Janet and Janelle who were my age. On my walks to school with the girls, we would pass by a gigantic oak tree on the corner, and there were strawberry fields across the street. During the summer months I would relish climbing that big oak; the branches were so huge you could wrap your arms around them and still not touch. I remember picking and eating the strawberries from the field, even though I was not supposed to do that. But, heck, the other kids did it, too, and the little Japanese man who owned the fields never complained.

Chapter Two: Déjà vu

From what I still remember, life as a child was simple, free and always fun. What I mean is it was carefree. Playing in the neighborhood was full of fun and surprises every single day. On my 8th birthday I was given a brand new Schwinn bicycle. It was purple and silver and definitely the envy of the neighborhood. I would ride it up and down the street pretending all the while that I was a dashing and daring motorcycle racer. Isn't that what all 8-year old boys are supposed to do? I attached playing cards to the front forks and held them in place with clothes pins (you won't remember those). The flapping sound they made when hitting the spokes sounded, to me anyway, like a motorcycle when I rode really fast. Well, I was riding really fast one afternoon and waiving to my friends as I swiftly swept by them when someone yelled. I looked over to see who it was and . . . Wham! I hit the back of a parked car and flew head-first into the tail lights splitting my forehead open, blood was everywhere. Shortly thereafter, I was introduced to stitches, about 10 of them as I recollect. That would not be the last of my "accidents." (Rags To Riches—Tony Bennett)

Many years later, while working at the Superior Court in Norwalk in the late 1970s, I spent one lunch hour on an enchanting adventure. With my trusty Thomas Guide (something else you won't remember) I searched for, found and drove to 11523 E. Brimley Street. With eager anticipation, I slowly rounded the corner and stopped for a minute in front of a small house that I'm sure was still filled with childhood memories.

The little white house looked just as it had when I was an adventurous and mischievous, fun-loving kid, exactly as I remembered it. A knock on the door brought a lovely, aging lady to my presence. I don't recall her name, sorry. She and her late husband bought the house when my family left in

1953. After explaining to her who I was and showing her my court ID, she graciously asked if I wanted to see the house. On entry, she led me through the small two bedroom house, but I was more interested in the back yard. It, too, was just like it was when I was a young boy living there. Well, almost. In the back, my dad's barbeque pit had been remodeled with a new enclosure and roof, but it was the same one I remembered. The long, narrow cement walk-way had been replaced by fancy paved stones. Wow! Goose-bumps covered my arms and a very melancholy mood captured me briefly. I softly smiled and thanked a warm and disarming lady for her gracious hospitality with a tender grasp of her hand covered by mine, and I left 11523 E. Brimley with my memories unaltered and a tear in my eye.

Occasionally, I recall that day with a warm glow. Until now, I have never told anyone about my adventure that day and my visit with a truly wonderful, charming lady, and I have never been back. Another chapter had closed.

> You might have heard my footsteps,
> Echo softly in the distance through the canyons of your mind.
> I might have even called your name
> As I ran searching after something to believe in . . .
>   . . . Bob Lind

Chapter 3: Always On The Move

While still in the third grade and living in Norwalk, something happened with my dad's business that greatly affected our family, and not in a good way. He owned and operated a Shell gas station on Beverly Blvd. in Montebello, California. I went there with him a few times, but didn't like it much. It was cold, greasy and left me feeling empty. One day at lunch I ate a pastrami sandwich from the little stand across the street from the station. Yuck! It made me sick. I haven't eaten pastrami since.

To this day, I am not aware of what happened with my dad's business. He never told me, but we lost our new house with the barbeque pit, the long cement walk-way, the green grass and the flower garden. We also lost my mom's beautiful, yellow Buick. I loved that car as I remember feeling safe and warm when riding in it. After that, my parents rarely seemed happy together and fought continually. The warmth and love of a close family had been shattered. Why was beyond me at that age and I never inquired when I grew older. We left Norwalk, my friends, my school and the strawberry fields. Our standard of living had crashed through the floor and the future would be a much more difficult place to endure.

Our move brought us to the city of Compton where we moved into an old dreary, run-down little house near the dry San Gabriel riverbed. There were bugs and mice everywhere and I would crunch them wherever I could. Present day Compton is viewed with scorn as a dangerous, pathetic place in South-Central Los Angeles. It wasn't much different then. It was an awful place in the white ghetto. A couple of bad "accidents" happened to me there. The first was totally my own stupid self, trying to impress the girls.

Two neighborhood sisters who liked playing with me and my dog accompanied us to the riverbed one afternoon where I showed them how to throw rocks. As I was showing off my new found skill, one of the rocks "accidently" hit one of the girls in the head causing it to bleed. Boy, did I get in trouble that night. The next day I was again down at the riverbed with the other sister and guess what happened? I hit her in the head with a rock! Can you believe that? Two days and two sisters with busted heads from my rocks. I couldn't believe my luck!

The second accident was not really an accident at all. It was an "on-purpose" and because of this one, we had to move again. My mom had bought me two little guinea pigs that I kept in the back yard in a small cement-brick enclosure. One was brown and the other was two-toned, brown and white. I built my little friends a "fort" out of small wooden boards from disassembling an orange crate (they don't make those anymore, either). Although it wasn't fancy, it had a small window on each side and a door in the front. One day while I was gathering grass and plants for them to eat, I noticed a head sticking out from under the shredded newspaper in the corner of the fort. My two Guinea pigs were eating the fresh salad I brought them and this other little head didn't make any sense. All of a sudden I had 3 Guinea pigs! I called my new little friend, "Squeaky." Life was good again.

Shortly, my tribe would grow to five. In the evenings, I would bring Squeaky in the house and as he sat on my lap, I would feed him greens I had freshly picked around the neighborhood that afternoon. Squeaky was my little buddy and he was oh so very, very friendly. His favorite play time was crawling up my arm and sitting on my shoulder and sniffing in my ear.

One afternoon while I was away at school, the boy who lived next door let his dog loose and it killed all my Guinea pigs. He thought it was very funny. My little, defenseless friends were scattered all around my back yard, each lying motionless. I cried and cried and cried. The next afternoon when I got home from school and was home alone, I loaded my dad's .22 rifle and shot the dog dead. Because of my antics, we were again forced to move away. I didn't like Compton anyway.

A small green and white house in El Monte was our next stop. I was still in the 3rd grade when something marvelous happened. While I was a bright kid, I was not a very good student. Baseball, tetherball, kickball, and just goofing off were on my menu every day. Mostly, I was good, very good, at getting in trouble. It was then that my third grade teacher, Mrs. Bailey, made quite an impression on me. She announced to her students that she would "reward" each of them if they got 100% on her weekly spelling tests. She would buy any student who got 100% an ice cream bar. My family was so poor we couldn't rub two nickels together and, of course, could not afford such luxuries. At that time an ice cream bar cost 5¢. The ones Mrs. Bailey bought were orange-flavored with vanilla ice cream in the middle and were called 50/50 bars. From that moment on, my study habits changed and I got 100% on every spelling test I took. Desert every Friday! In fact, I scored at or near the top of my class in any test I took. By discovering a way to develop pride in myself, I decided then and there that if I was going to do something, I would be the best at it. Period. The future wasn't as bleak as it once seemed. It wasn't long, though, that we moved again, no more ice cream bars.

Our now dysfunctional family soon settled in Baldwin Park, California. My head is filled with clouded memories of living in a small, dark brown house on Syracuse Avenue with the San Gabriel River behind us. At that time, there were neither any freeways nor any cement channels for water run-off in the river. I spent many days exploring the riverbed catching lizards, horned toads and small snakes. It was great fun as I entertained myself with creatures.

Then one morning when I was 10 years old, I sort of had another accident. On Easter Sunday, I was playing on the swings and showing off to the other kids when I suddenly flipped out backwards, landing very awkwardly, breaking my left arm just above the wrist. I didn't actually fall out; I was practicing jumping out of the swing backwards and crashed. Dumb, huh? Because we had little money and no insurance (who had insurance in those days), I was taken to the charity ward at County General Hospital in Los Angeles where my arm was placed in a plaster cast. We had to wait from about 10:00 a.m. until well after dark to see a doctor. My mom bought me a hotdog from a vending machine for a quarter. It came in a round tube. She jokingly told me if I could put my broken arm in the tube, we could just go home. I was hurting badly and my mom was trying to cheer me up. She was really sweet. That unpleasant experience lasted for 8 weeks. Every evening I would break off straws from our broom just to scratch the itch that was continually under that stupid cast. When it finally came off, I freaked as my left arm looked about the size of a toothpick.

During my 10th year in the summer of 1955, a fourth child was born to our family. Terry Nicholas Steven bounced into this world on July 2nd. Had he waited just two more days, his birthday would have been a yearly "bang." As I remember, Terry was an inquisitive kid, always eager to explore and try new ideas. I fondly remember him as a youngster trying to ride a unicycle, falling off and crashing into everything. I would laugh at him and just shake my head thinking . . . stupid brother. After a great deal of practice and several bumps and bruises, he could ride it really well. I was impressed and praised him for his miracle accomplishment and thought I would try it. Not good! Boom! Flat on my butt. Shortly thereafter Terry became a master cyclist and he could stop, go, turn and jump at will. It was then that I began to realize and understand that everyone has talent, probably different from your own.

What I remember most about my littlest brother was his constant borrowing of money. "Hey, big brother, can you loan me a couple bucks?" later became, "Can I borrow a twenty?" I don't ever remember him paying me back, but it didn't matter. I had become his private bank.

Soon we moved back to El Monte, near Durfee and Rush Road. I attended Monte Vista Elementary School in the 5th grade where I played lots of baseball and got pretty good at it, too. One Saturday on game day, I noticed a girl in the bleachers. Her name was Donna Hammond and she was in my 5th grade class. She clapped and yelled for me! Imagine that? Donna wasn't my first girlfriend, but she was the first girl I liked. The next morning, Donna was riding a white horse down our street. She stopped and asked if I wanted to ride one, too. Her parents owned a riding stable and Donna invited me to come over and perhaps ride one of the horses. I learned to ride horses with her and it didn't cost a cent (sort of). I was her friend and her dad let me hang around the stables, helping now and then. That's where I learned how to sling manure.

While living in El Monte, I made the little league all-star team. School was okay, but not as much fun as baseball. I decided if I was ever going to college I would major in baseball. Thinking back, I still remember one little league game where I hit 2 grand slam home runs and we lost 9-8. My friends and I were always playing baseball (over-the-line). Actually, I can't remember any time as a youngster when I wasn't playing baseball. Saturdays were especially fun as our over-the-line games started early, around 9:00 o'clock in the morning, and went 'til early evening. All-day baseball every Saturday.

In the evenings, I would listen to music on an old, red plastic radio. The dial was gold-colored and cracked and finding a station to lock onto was almost impossible. My mom didn't watch television since we didn't own one, so she listened to my radio during the day. Those years are a mere blur to me now, except for mom's singing. Mostly, I remember playing baseball and the joy it brought to me. Before long, we moved again.

Chapter 4: I'm Rich!

Our next stop was back to Baldwin Park while I was in the 6th grade. School was alright, I guess, but I don't ever remember doing homework. Why would I do homework when I could play baseball? Besides, I did very well on any test I took. School was just too easy. I had a neighbor friend named Eddie. He wasn't very bright, but he had a fast, red and green go-cart that I got to ride a lot until I crashed it against the curb and a truck. Another Oops!

One Saturday, Eddie came to one of my little league games. I was joking with him when he pulled a coin out of his pocket. I had never seen a coin like it. What was it, I wondered? So I asked him. He didn't know. Neither did I. When asked if he wanted to sell it he said no, but he would give it to me if I hit a home run that day. Easy money! I was collecting coins at the time and I owned a small Lincoln cent collection, along with Jefferson and Buffalo nickel collections, and a Mercury dime collection. Quarter collections cost too much so I had none of those. I didn't own any valuable coins, but I did have a 1909-S, a 1914-S, and a 1931-D penny, and a 1938-D Buffalo nickel. I kept them in those old blue, three-fold Whitman coin albums. In those days, finding old coins was not difficult and I spent hours and hours 'exchanging' change at the store to search out the really hard-to-find gems. The coin Eddie gave me was different. It looked like a mercury dime, but it was larger (about the size of a nickel) and was gold colored. It was dated 1883 and on the back it said Five D. It was a $5 gold piece, but I didn't know it. (Tammy—Debbie Reynolds)

The next Monday I took my new coin to the "Antique" lady (that's what we called her) who owned and operated a coin shop on Ramona Boulevard in Baldwin Park and sold lots of junk stuff besides coins. I was often in her tiny shop with my buddies trying to sell or trade her our "gems" that were not worth much. She had all the old red coin books that told how much the Lincoln cents, Buffalo and Jefferson Nickels, and the others were worth. She was kind and patient and enjoyed having the kids drop in on her to explore the coin books. Looking back, she was probably a little lonely and enjoyed the company of the neighborhood kids. She greeted me as always by saying, "Hello, Steven, what have you today?" Today, however, would be different.

I pulled the coin Eddie gave me out of my pocket and handed it to her. She examined the coin closely and asked if I wanted to sell it? I asked her in a bold, authoritative voice, "How much?" Her reply stunned me. She looked at me quizzically for the longest time and sheepishly asked if I would take $27.50. (For $27.50, I couldn't say yes fast enough, but I didn't let her know that.) She was slow to offer, so I took my time. After a few lingering moments, I asked her if she thought that was a fair price. She said, "For an average $5 gold piece, I believe it's fair." The coin was a $5 gold piece from 1883! I had no idea. Wow! $27.50! I was rich!

That was more money than I ever had. My entire coin collection wasn't worth that much. I scooped up the cash and went across the street to the local neighborhood store. It was appropriately named the "Grab and Run" market on Ramona Boulevard. I bought 2 candy bars, an ice cream cone and a Pepsi, total 30¢. Since I had so much money I bought some pork chops for dinner and headed home. On arriving I told my mom what had happened and gave her the rest of the money, about $25. I had no idea of the value of $27.50. I mean, it was 1956 and I was just an innocent kid. Actually, I was a little apprehensive about having all that cash so I gave it to the one person I cared for the most—my mom. She never questioned me about it and I saw a little relief in her face when I handed the money over to her. She gave me a warm smile and hugged me. Our family lived on the ropes and the money was a real windfall. Giving it to her made me feel proud and I beamed a broad smile. Dinner that evening tasted especially good.

That year we moved again and again, always landing somewhere in El Monte or Baldwin Park. I guess it wasn't easy finding a place to rent with four kids and a dog. I remember when we moved to Rivergrade Road in

El Monte where I attended the 7th grade. I tried to locate that house once, but it was no longer there, replaced by an industrial park. Although the house was gone, the memories are not. It was there where I had my first, but not last, broken heart.

On a cold and wet Saturday morning a truck drove by the house and hit my dog, breaking her ribs. She was whining and whimpering; I was crying. She died in my arms and I have never forgotten that heartfelt moment. I was truly saddened, but there wasn't much time to dwell on it, though. School was starting soon.

Ethel D. Keenan Junior High School is where I learned to say cuss words, but I didn't know what they meant. My mom had protected her children well and I was very naive, but didn't want the other kids to know it. My sister attended an elementary school close to Keenan and I would walk her to school in the mornings. My brothers were too young for school.

At Keenan I made lots of new friends. On reflection, making friends always came easy to me. My new best friend was named Scott. He was the fastest kid in school and bragged about it all the time. One day while playing flag football, Scotty broke loose and was going for a touchdown when I caught him from behind and pulled his flag. "No touchdown today," I cheerfully told him. Later in the game I ran for a touchdown with Scotty on my heels, but he never caught me. There was a new fastest kid in school and Scotty wasn't him.

While attending Keenan, I started to notice the new creatures walking around the hallways. They were called girls. I was still terribly shy, and Scotty and I had many talks about girls. Since he knew everything about girls, I listened intently. One day after school Scotty and I were walking home together talking about baseball and this girl named Sharon was teasing us about something. She was a pretty brunette and Scotty started talking to her and after a few minutes he was "kissing" her on the mouth. Can you believe that? I walked home in disgust.

Our next door neighbor on Rivergrade Road had a bunch of kids, all younger than me except Larry, a little red-headed squirt with lots of freckles, my age, who was always pestering Ginger. One morning when we were walking to school, Larry said something nasty to Ginger that made her cry. I walked up to him and he said he wasn't afraid of me. The next thing he knew he was on the ground nursing a busted lip and bawling like a baby. I hugged my little sister and told her everything was okay. Ginger and I argued a lot, but she was my sister.

Following the 7th grade, we moved again, back to Baldwin Park. This time it was an old, broken-down, faded red house on Salisbury Street not far from Ramona Boulevard and the San Gabriel River. For the 8th grade, I was enrolled at Charles D. Jones Junior High School. As usual, I made new friends and started to excel in sports. My home room was in the wood shop building, and my wood shop class was the period right after lunch. One of the boys in my home room usually brought his lunch to school. One day he brought a bottle of grape juice to have with lunch. During wood shop that day, he got real sick and barfed. My teacher, Mr. Butterbaugh, was not happy as he escorted the kid to the nurse's office. Seems his grape juice wasn't grape juice after all, it was burgundy. Oops! (It's All In The Game—Tommy Edwards)

There would be no more moving. Baldwin Park became our hometown and I would attend the same high school for 4 years. Wow! Imagine that. Roots.

Chapter 5: Learning About Music

My education made a huge leap in the 8th grade, for the most part because of math and music. Mr. Smith was my teacher for 7th period math class. I thought of him as some sort of genius, and he was. He taught his students square roots and how to solve them long-hand. I learned a great deal about algebra and geometry from him and he taught it in such a way that math became easy, but more than that it was fun! He made it fun because he was always smiling and telling you that numbers were related and it was just a game, like a puzzle, to figure them out.

By the end of the school year, Mr. Smith had introduced me and several of my friends to Rock 'n Roll music. Oh, I had heard plenty of songs on the radio over the years, mostly country and pop. At some point, I don't remember exactly when, my mom mentioned her favorite song was an old standard by Sammy Turner called Lavender Blue. My memory of songs went back much further than that, though, and whenever a song came on the radio that I really liked, I would search the airways for hours just to hear it over and over and over again. Life was free and easy and I reveled in the music I listened to on the radio. (Lavender Blue—Sammy Turner)

Sammy Turner

One day, to my surprise, mom bought me a record player. I would start a record collection that would carry on through the 1980s, when records would be replaced by cassette tapes.

Music became my invisible friend and a safe haven where I could retreat while coming of age. How Much Is That Doggie In The Window (Patti Page) and other Pop songs on the radio like You, You, You (The Ames Brothers) from 1953 bring back fond memories of my time on Brimley Street. Other songs like Hey There (Rosemary Clooney), Secret Love (Doris Day), and the song many consider the 1st Rock & Roll song Sh-Boom (The Crew Cuts) helped me dream during my lost and unhappy period in the late 1950s. The wonderful sounds pouring out of the radio would help a young teenager cope during the turbulent times that were on the horizon, and now that I had a record machine, well, I could explore the new possibilities . . . No matter how happy or sad I would be, listening to the music I loved always made me smile, even in the worst of times.

Mr. Smith knew a great deal about Rock 'n Roll music as he was a DJ on the weekends and he often told us captivating stories about the different artists on the records he played. A few of us would hang out in Mr. Smith's classroom after school and listen to his stories. I didn't realize it then, but telling stories would become my way of communicating with others throughout my life. It's the best way to teach and the easiest way to learn; nothing tells it better than a good story. Not surprisingly, I have so many stories locked away and almost all relate to music. Probably without knowing it, those songs on the radio helped ease the pain of childhood and the transition to becoming a teenager and the heartaches that were yet to come. (Lonely Teenager—Dion)

Chapter 6: Crushing Heartache

There were other, much more dramatic events during my 8th grade year at Jones. I played on the football team as a half-back and receiver. Because I had a strong arm and was a very accurate passer, I wanted to play quarterback, but we had a quarterback named Leon Kidwell who threw the football like a bullet, very, very hard, and he was a fantastic football player and a good friend. Besides, I could outrun anyone once I was in the clear. Leon walked around school with a quiet arrogance that I envied, and I was practically the only one who could catch his passes. I must have been since I scored EVERY touchdown in EVERY game. Our 8th grade football team never lost. Got to confess, though, we only played six games. After our final game against Landis Junior High School on Tuesday, November 4, 1958, I was walking home singing It's Only Make Believe (Conway Twitty) and joking to myself. It was the #1 song in the country, we had won our final football game 12-0, and I was on top of the world, but not for long.

I was almost home when a familiar car pulled up next to me. My uncle Johnny was driving and told me to get in the car. He was usually a jovial guy, but he was sternly serious this day. A couple of my cousins were also in the car, yet nobody spoke to me. That was unusually out of character, but I was still "up" from the afternoon's events and wanted to talk about my football game, yet everyone was so sullen. When we got to my house, the place was full of relatives. They all looked so sad; many of my aunts and cousins were crying. Bewildered, I was ushered out to the back yard where my dad was talking to some relatives and neighbors. They all left and when we were alone my dad silently took me by the shoulders and looked in my eyes. A few moments later a tear ran down his face as he told me that my sister, Ginger, had died that morning. I said or asked, "Is Ginger dead?" I was crushed. This was just not real.

For the past few days I had been feeling listless like I was fighting off a cold, but it wasn't that bad. Besides, I had a football game to play. Ginger was also feeling poorly and she would often weep softly. I remember she didn't get out of bed that morning. She had stayed home from school the day before and she pleaded with my mom to stay home from school again. What did stupid Steven say? I told my mom that Ginger was faking so she wouldn't have to go to school. The last thing I ever said to my little sister was, "You're a faker," as I walked out the door. Now I felt like I was 2 inches tall. My little sister was gone, cheated out of life by diphtheria, one of hand-full of death cases reported in the U.S. in 1958. I never got the chance to say good-bye to her. Here I was, 13 years old and enveloped in ceaseless, gut-wrenching guilt. The walls started going up. (A Letter To An Angel—Jimmy Clanton)

Letter To An Angel

Not only did I fall into an emotional pit, I brought a shovel with me and buried myself. I did not attend my sister's funeral. I couldn't. Instead, I ran away at age 13 and stayed gone for several days until the Sheriff found me at the riverbed. I slept there in one of the cavities under a bridge overpass. Cold, hungry, miserable and very alone, there was no resistance when they found me. The weight of the world was crushing me and I couldn't escape; I didn't know how. Months would pass before another smile crossed my face. 1958 was not a good year and 1962 wouldn't be any better. I would be a very angry and hurting young man throughout my teenage years.

For those and other reasons I had yet to understand, I was involved in many altercations during my turbulent teen years, winning some and not-so-winning others. I never walked away from an argument. Never. I became defiant and would stay in that condition for a very long time.

Why was life so hard? It was a question I asked myself over and over, yet, because of my age, I didn't realize it was not the right question. I would learn later that feeling sorry for myself was not the answer, either. The right question would have been: "Steven, you've been dealt a bad hand, what are you going to do about it?" John Wayne said it best, "Life is hard, it's even harder if you're stupid."

Chapter 7: Starting High School

Most of the memories after my sister died until September 1959, when I started high school at BPHS, are lost to me. During that summer a new bowling center opened in our city. Named Baldwin Park Bowl, I would spend countless hours there learning a new sport. I was still locked away in guilt and very troubled when I started high school, but found solace in my studies, in sports, and in music. By that time, I had discovered a way to disguise my feelings: I would be the voice on the radio that no one could see, but more than that, no one knew me and no one got close. Closeness always seemed to bring a great deal of pain with it, so I avoided the pain. Frankie Avalon, Lloyd Price, Roy Orbison, and The Fleetwoods dominated the radio airways, and they were my invisible friends. I watched 77 Sunset Strip on television and had a crush on Cricket Blake (Connie Stevens). She was a goofy, blue-eyed blonde, but she was gorgeous, funny, and she laughed a lot. And she could sing.

Laughter became a cure for all ailments and it gave me the opportunity to 'lighten up' and relax. I could be anyone I wanted to be, because, like my mom, I was a dreamer. There was nothing or no one I couldn't be. Just listen to the radio . . .

I made many new friends at BPHS: Jim Pratt, Dave Frame, Darrel Foster, Henry Dock, and Paul Rouse, names that mean nothing to anyone at this point, except your dad. They are part of me, and for what it's worth, part of my personality. Jim and I hung out together and we were always competing with each other. As a freshman, he set a school record by doing 600 sit-ups in 30 minutes, but he couldn't play basketball very well. I ran him all over the court. He and I ran cross-country together and he was the one who got me interested in bowling.

Dave Frame was the only person kicked out of school (suspended) his freshman year for smoking a cigarette in the boys restroom. That was about as bad as it got in high school, nothing like it is today. Dave would go on to become a member of the PBA (Professional Bowlers Association) and he won a few tournaments. Framer (what I called him) was sharp and quick when it came to current music titles; we would have mental jousts trying to out-do one another. More than that, he enjoyed playing practical jokes and I was usually the gullible one.

Darrel Foster was a pool hustler and a very, very good one. Also, he was a butcher's intern at Stater Bros. Market while in high school. One day at school he bragged that he had $100 cash on him. I bet him a nickel he didn't; it was all the money I had. He opened his wallet containing 5 twenties and smiled as he took my nickel and put it in his pocket. Darrel always used a quirky expression when someone asked him a question and he knew the answer. He would very slowly say, "Whyyyyyyyy, certainly." He was a good friend, yet never had the opportunity to establish a relationship with a woman (that I am aware) as he had two invalid parents he cared for all his life. I lost track of Darrel in the mid-1980s. He was one of the good guys.

Henry Dock and I became friends and studied math and calculus together on our lunch breaks. Henry would go on to become a police officer for the Baldwin Park Police Department and later a detective for the City of Bell Gardens Police Department. My fondest memories of Henry were of him laughing. He did that a lot and he did it loudly. And he liked beer! Those were excellent qualities.

Paul Rouse was a year younger than me, yet he would become my very best and closest friend for several years. We would argue for hours over who was shafted the most in life. His mother had been raped as a teenager and Paul was the outcome of that attack. Later, because she couldn't cope, she left him with his grandparents. When he moved in with them, they changed his last name to Adamcik. Paul had a heart condition and one day after school, while playing football, I threw a hard pass to him from about 20 yards away that hit him square in the chest and he went down. I was scared to death, but, thankfully, it only knocked the wind out of him. I never threw Paul another pass and he let me know he was not happy about that. To make up for it, Paul would one day introduce me to his new girlfriend, another turning point in my life.

Although I participated in several sports in high school: football, basketball, baseball, track, and cross-country, I spent most of my free time reading and studying, until I discovered bowling. Not only did I love this new sport, I became good at it. Really good. No, that's not the right word. That's not what I mean. I became exceptional at it. I started hanging out at Baldwin Park Bowl doing odd jobs for the proprietors so I could bowl for free. No job was too small or too difficult, and I did anything and everything: picked up trash in the parking lot, emptied ash trays, swept the floor, just about anything. I made sure I did all my homework at school and then headed to BP Bowl in the early afternoons. Most of the time, Jim (Pratt) was there, too. He was better than me, but not for long. My first year bowling I averaged 186 and had a high game of 268! Not bad for a 15 year old kid. None of the other junior bowlers even came close. By the age of 16, I was averaging over 200 and was very, very conceited. Actually I was not conceited, I was convinced. Conceit was a fault and, obviously, I had no faults. I was an egotistical disaster waiting to happen. (Cathy's Clown—Everly Brothers)

Chapter 8: Out of the Past

Occasionally my mom came to the lanes to watch me bowl; my dad never did. Mom tried it with me once and to my pleasant surprise, she was pretty good. I was amazed at her grace (no pun intended) and coordination. Amazingly, mom was quite an athlete and when I told her so she just smiled and hugged me. After our game, we were sitting in the coffee shop having a soda when she was suddenly and very shockingly surprised.

A lady came into the coffee shop said, "Hi, Steven." My mom stared at her breathlessly. Bewildered, I asked if she knew Dottie, the lady who came in. They just stared at each other for the longest time, then mom stood up and they hugged each other. It turns out my mom and Dottie were very close friends as teenagers, but had lost contact. They started talking and hours went by and Dottie told my mom that I was her "scorekeeper" for her ladies bowling team on Monday nights.

Most evenings I would keep score for the bowling leagues to make money to bowl. At that time, junior bowlers were charged just 25¢ a game. Each league bowler paid the scorekeeper 25¢. If there were 10 bowlers, that meant $2.50. I usually made more (tips) since I was very neat with numbers and the people seemed to like me, even if I was a little snot most of the time. On most Friday and Saturday nights I kept score for both the 6:00 and 9:00 o'clock leagues. Because I practiced more than 50 games a week, I became very accurate. Remember, I have a bad right eye. Left-eye dominance is an asset to a right-handed bowler or so I was told.

My first year in high school was fairly uneventful for the most part. Sure, I received superlative grades, participated in several sports, and bowled. My favorite pastime, though, was listening to the radio. I had a transistor radio (you guys have no idea what I'm talking about) that costs $3. Rock 'n Roll music was evolving and I really enjoyed the transition. The music then was pure and innocent, and had very catchy lyrics, nothing like much of today's rubbish. The lyrics contained no swearing, no vulgarity, no sexual innuendoes and no words of violence. Memories of "The night was clear and the moon was yellow . . . ," from Stagger Lee (Lloyd Price) and "Going to Kansas City, Kansas City here I come . . . ," from Kansas City (Wilbert Harrison) still ring true in my ears. Near the end of the school year, the radio DJs would continually play Here Comes Summer (Jerry Keller) to set the mood for teenagers and the fun that was yet to be enjoyed. Life in 1959-61 (my first high school years) was carefree and carried an innocence with it that will never be recaptured. Unfortunately, the time of youthful innocence was close to being gone forever.

As a young teenager growing up in an uncomplicated world, I wasn't very sophisticated socially. I was often confused in social situations and I was usually uncertain on how to behave. I stepped on my lips so many times that I started to 'clam up' around girls, unless I already knew them. Then I would just make a fool of myself. I made lots of mistakes, lots of blunders. I said things I should never have said and did things I laugh about now. Man, for a smart kid, I was pretty dumb and acted like it. My mom tried to teach me what she could, but I was rebellious and acted like I already knew everything. One thing that lingered with me was my own peaceful turmoil (my sister) that I shared with no one. My dad wasn't around much and the close family unit I knew as a youngster no longer existed. My mom wasn't carefree anymore and she no longer sang songs to us. She seemed empty and very alone. I knew she missed her daughter and I would often find her weeping softly when I came home from school, but it wasn't only missing Ginger that made her cry. (Wings Of A Dove—Ferlin Husky)

After my sister passed, mom insisted on moving out of the house where Ginger died. We moved next door when that house became available. It was a scrubby, small, white two-bedroom shack with a covered screen porch in front and lots of trees. Out in the back was a newly constructed garage that the owner had put in. There were several old cars in the back that didn't run. One day I asked my mom if I could live in the garage and she agreed, but only if I behaved. I was free. I swept out the garage, put my bed in it and set up my own private world. I had the record machine my mom had purchased from McMahan's Furniture in Baldwin Park, and I had a little desk and a lamp so I could do my homework (if I had any). As long as I didn't get into any trouble, I was allowed to come and go as I pleased without supervision.

I was a tall, skinny kid as a freshman, standing 5"10" and a meek 125 pounds when I started high school. By the time I graduated I was 6'3" and a brisk 175. Playing on the JV basketball team, I scored 17 points in a game against powerful Muir High School in South Pasadena. We lost that game 41-17. Got that! Our team wasn't very good; we won only 3 or 4 games that year. As a sophomore I finished 2nd in the CIF Southern Section Cross-Country finals at Mt. San Antonio College in Walnut, finishing the two mile mountain course in 9:30 (Mr. Pratt finished 5th). Also as a sophomore, during a league track meet, I ran the mile in 4:32 and had a promising future as a distance runner, but I really wasn't interested. I was quite an athlete, but still incredibly shy around girls. Oh, there were a few I really liked, but I made sure none of them ever knew.

I had a crush on Sandy Wise who was a straight "A" student I met in CSF (California Scholastic Federation). To join CSF, your grades had to be stellar. Mine were. I remember an advanced English class where the teacher, Mrs. Geisler, read one of my essays aloud in class. She said I had a gift with words. Man, was I ever embarrassed. That same scenario would happen in college. Fortunately, I missed that class, but my fellow students were all over me about it. Back to Sandy: She was a pretty brunette with amazingly green eyes. Me? I was an oak, a perfect statue. Sandy never knew me, but I dated her in dreams. Mostly, I just watched her as she walked by me in the hall. (Will You Love Me Tomorrow—Shirelles)

Rock music in 1961 brought new sounds. The Motown sound was evolving with groups like The Shirelles and The Marvelettes. Elvis was always around it seemed, but new vigor entered Rock with Del Shannon and Dion. I tried, at a dare, a new sport—roller skating. My cousin Paul Gardner (remember him, born in the same bed as me only 2 months earlier) talked me into it and together we would frequent the Skylark Roller Rink in Baldwin Park on Friday and Saturday nights. I was venturing out into the world with anticipation and wonder. I had no idea what to expect, but I wanted to explore all the avenues. Skating was fun for many reasons, especially the music they played while skating. My best friend, Paul Adamcik, would join in the festivities. He could literally dance on skates. Me? I just wanted to go fast; I loved speed. When we weren't skating, we would sit around one of the tables competing in arm wrestling. Good ol' cousin Paul dominated. He had arms like tree trunks. A few of my other cousins started skating and for a while, most of the kids at the rink were my relatives. We were quite an awkward group. After a while, skating became boring, but I would return to it later for a very different reason.

As I started my sophomore year in high school, my bowling career was on the move up. Adamcik was not a bad bowler and we had a pretty good junior team. There were five of us that entered a junior traveling league as the team from Baldwin Park Bowl. Jim Pratt, Paul Adamcik, Steve Chatlovsky, Marshall Goldsmith and myself comprised the team. I was the anchor (5th bowler). The anchor on a team is generally considered the top bowler on the team and the best under pressure. I averaged 195 that year—tops in the league.

Many things happened in 1962 that have never left my memories. How could they? My mom came to see me bowl regularly and asked when I was going to bowl a 300 (perfect) game for her. I would tell her, "One of these days, mom, one of these days . . ."

Chapter 9: Devastation

In early April of my junior year, I was summoned out of class by one of the school teachers, Mr. Tankersley. He was my 1st period algebra teacher and got a great deal of pleasure from giving me 'detention.' There must have been some days when I wasn't late, just can't remember any. He informed me that my mother had been taken to the hospital and he gave me a ride home. My dad was already home from his job at Shell Oil. Several of my relatives were also there. I was apprized that my mom had suffered a stroke of some kind and was at Lark Ellen Hospital in West Covina. I went to the hospital to see her, but she wasn't awake. She seemed to be sleeping peacefully.

During the time my mom was in a coma, my imagination ran wild. Her recovery was all important to her children, especially to Kim and Terry, my younger brothers. Two days later, on Thursday, April 5, 1962, my worst fears and concerns were actualized. My mom passed away from a ruptured cerebral aneurysm. Life had stopped cold once again and, once again, the walls went up, much stronger than before. I still had much to learn about life not being fair. (Stranger on the Shore—Mr. Acker Bilk)

No school for a while. No nothing for a while. No friends. Nothing. I called Baldwin Park Bowl on Monday evening and told Dottie I wouldn't be keeping score that night and she asked my why. When I told her that my mom had died, she fainted. I attended my mom's funeral at Rose Hills Memorial Park in Whittier. I probably started a river as I sat next to my mom's casket for the longest time, until everyone had left. Only then in my solitude did I say my final good-bye. She was buried next to my sister. It just didn't seem fair that I should lose the ones closest to me. It just wasn't fair. And because I was so young and immature, I didn't realize there were others hurting as badly as me.

I was 17 years old and I thought I was much stronger than when my sister passed away. Stupid me, I was the same old mush bucket. The only difference this time is that I didn't blame myself and I had made it a point to stay close to my mom as I grew. Although I was ordinarily extremely gregarious, I remained solemn for weeks. I went through the motions of doing the things that interested me, but it was difficult, so very difficult.

Those feelings have been spared you two and I am grateful for that in my own way; the hurt of losing a loved one, especially when you're an innocent and confused child, is a very lonely, helpless and empty emotion.

Remembering those feelings helped me a great deal understanding Alicia's emotions and the essay she had written for her dad because of them. My most vivid memory of my hospital stay was of Alicia standing guard over me. At such a young age, I was yet to discover that love fills the glass; loss empties it. I had a table of empty glasses. (All Alone Am I—Brenda Lee)

Chapter 10: Moving On

Shortly after my mom left us alone and lonely, I noticed a change in my little brothers. They were emotionally lost as if they were little zombies wondering aimlessly around the house, hopelessly mesmerized in silence. I wasn't much better and since I had no experience in life, except for losing my sister a few years before, just sitting with them seemed to work, but only for a while. Had I known that talking with them and discussing what had happened to our mom and sister would have helped ease the burden on us, I would have poured it all out. Of course, I just didn't know. How could I? The three of us silently struggled with our emotions for years.

To ease the pain of a staggering loss and assist my shrinking family, I got a job washing dishes at the coffee shop at Baldwin Park Bowl @ $1.25 an hour. As a bonus, I was allowed to have a meal before I started and a meal at for lunch in the middle of my shift. After work, I was allowed another meal, but I always got my last meal to go and took it home. Usually, it was a club sandwich or a hamburger & fries that could be shared. My little brothers enjoyed the "donated" meals I brought them. On reflection, the meal deals were most likely given to me to help out; it was a kind gesture from some very caring individuals which took me years to understand.

I was anxiously looking forward to my first paycheck and when I got it (about $90 for 2 weeks) I cashed it and put the money in my wallet. My dad had insisted that I give him my paycheck since we really needed the money for expenses and that was okay with me; I was glad I could help. Well, that didn't happen. Someone picked my pocket or I lost my wallet somewhere. In any event, I didn't have the money and my dad was furious. What could I say or do? Nothing, that's what. But he didn't relent and I was bombarded with verbal abuse and torment by an apparently uncaring and unforgiving father I never grew close to. Since that day, I have never carried a wallet.

By May, there were several leagues I bowled in that were ending. On the last night of league bowling there is a sweepstakes where bowlers put money in a pot for singles (your score), doubles (yours + another bowler's score), and team event (highest score of each team). What that means is the person who bowls best on the last night has a chance to make some good money. At that time I was bowling incredibly well and I raked in the cash, about $400 overall for all the leagues I bowled. I put it all in an envelope and handed it to my dad and told him it was for mom's funeral expenses. He took the money silently. (Crying In The Rain—The Everly Brothers)

It was May before I started coming out of my shell and my bowling took off, probably because I was more focused on it and not much else. On Sunday afternoon, May 27, 1962, I was bowling in a pot game at Baldwin Park Bowl where everyone participating puts in money, usually $5, and bowls one game across 12 lanes with the highest score taking the "pot." For this particular game, I was the lead-off bowler on the telescore (a clear acetate sheet projected onto a scoreboard). There were 14 bowlers in the game so the pot was worth $70. I started the game innocently enough with a strike, then another, and another and another. Soon I had the first 8 strikes in a row and people started congregating behind me. After the 9th strike, a loud cheer went up. I was surprised by all the attention and I felt something special was about to happen. After strikes 10 and 11 the cheering grew louder and louder. One more strike to go for a perfect 300 game. Baldwin Park Bowl had been open for 3 years and there had never been a perfect 300 game rolled there. When I stood on the approach for the 12th and final delivery, I took a deep breath and relaxed. You could have heard a pin drop. Was I nervous? Not in the least. I had rehearsed this moment hundreds of times in my mind. Just before the last shot I murmured to myself, "Mama, this one's for you." I took my approach and released the ball knowing all too well the final outcome. Before the ball hit the pins, I turned away and walked back toward the settee area as an explosion of cheers went up. I had just bowled the first 300 game ever at Baldwin Park Bowl. If only my mom could have been there. I realize this sounds a bit conceited, but it really isn't. I had a great deal of confidence in my abilities, and when you do something correctly and repetitiously over an extended length of time, you become superior at it. I excelled at bowling, simply stated.

That Sunday was a clear, warm and bright sunshine day. The #1 song in the country on that date was Stranger On The Shore (Mr. Acker Bilk) and whenever I hear that song and its soft melody, I remember that memorable afternoon of May 27, 1962. It was both a sad and happy day, but one that is forever etched in my mind. Sad as I reminisce at times and picture my mom being there, beaming a proud smile. Happy because my life was about to change for the better as I was about to discover love for the first time.

People were congratulating me and my best friend, Paul Adamcik, came up to me smiling and extending his hand to congratulate me. He had a girl with him. Paul and I shook hands and he introduced me to his girlfriend. Her name was Charmaine Saxton. She lived in West Covina and attended West Covina High School as a sophomore. Paul had met her at the Skylark Roller Rink a few weeks earlier. She was a cute girl with blue eyes, blonde hair and a warm glow. She smiled and when we made eye contact, I was hooked, instantly. Wow! What a feeling!

Charmaine

I started skating again the next weekend just to see her. Within a couple months she would become my first girlfriend and would remain so until I was drafted into the U.S. Army in April 1966. Why did it take a couple months? Well, I was still shy around girls and it took me a couple months to get up the courage to see her.

Shortly after Charmaine and I became an item, a new rock group hit the airways with a dazzling, captivating sound. They called themselves The Four Seasons and their lead singer, Frankie Valli, was a high tone, much like Ritchie Valens, only much smoother. His sparkling, clear voice was unmistakable and The Four Seasons recorded hit after hit until the late sixties when the group broke up and Frankie Valli went on to a very successful solo career.

The Four Seasons first charted song was "Sherry" and it would also become their first #1 song, and since Charmaine was my first girl, I nick-named her "Sherry." Many years later (2006), a Broadway musical production entitled The Jersey Boys would entertain the new generation (and the old alike) with music courtesy of The Four Seasons. The production was so successful, it toured the country. The Four Seasons was my favorite musical group until 1966 when a group of four very talented, yet diverse folk singers formed a folk/rock group whose popularity would capture the country. (Sherry—The Four Seasons)

For the first time, at age 17, I had a girlfriend and her presence helped ease my heavy heart. For once in a very long time, I felt warmth. On my first date with Charmaine we traveled to the Los Angeles County Fair in Pomona. I didn't have a car so we took the bus. Very romantic, huh?

When I did get my first car, it was a real beauty. It was a faded blue, 1953 Mercury, solid rust inside and out. I paid $10 for it, but it ran. It used lots of oil and the radiator leaked. Thank goodness bulk oil costs just 10¢ a quart back then and water for the radiator was free. When I washed it, it still looked dingy. The head liner was old, torn and faded so I ripped it out, didn't need it anyway I thought. The radio worked so I had music. It was a piece of junk, but it was my junk and I was proud of it.

Being mobile meant I could travel to different bowling centers to complete in the games. I was still a junior in high school when I started bowling in a tournament called the King of the Hill. The object of the tournament was to get as many strikes as possible in three games. Score didn't count, only strikes did. It usually took about 16 or 17 strikes to come out on top. After the preliminaries, the person who finished on top with the most strikes got to bowl the current King of the Hill, one game with the one getting the most strikes being crowned "king" for a week until the next tournament. A prize of $25 was given the king; the runner-up got $15. The King of the Hill remained king until he was beaten, and because he was the reigning king, he didn't have to go through the preliminaries. The tournament usually took place on a Saturday. At one point I was King of the Hill at both Baldwin Park Bowl and Covina Bowl at the same time! That meant $50 a week for a couple weeks anyway. I didn't stay king very long, but it was fun while it lasted.

During the week, I would still keep score to make money. After that summer, I wasn't in the coffee shop washing dishes anymore either. Out of necessity I had become a hustler and I gave money each morning to my little brothers for school lunches. I didn't always have much, but I gave it to them anyway. They were just 7 and 9 years old. Thinking back on it, I don't know how we survived as well as we did. Like other families in our position, we found a way to trudgingly "get through it."

We moved away from Salisbury Street to another dreary old house on Mangum Avenue a few blocks away, still in Baldwin Park, though. We lived in the back house on a two-house lot with only the barest of necessities. After a couple weeks my brothers made friends with the kids next door who were around their age. There always seemed to be lots of kids around our house. It was a busy place. One day I met the neighbor kids' mother. Her name was Dolores; she was a seamstress at some clothing manufacturing outfit in the area. Her children were Terry, Mike, Craig and Vanessa. Vanessa was just a baby, perhaps 2 years old. I became very fond of Vanessa and we would play together, always laughing and having a good time. Vanessa was a darling little child, and she and I formed a very close bond (I wonder why?).

A few months later, my dad bought a new house on Waco Street in Baldwin Park. The house was some sort of "private deal" as one of my mom's sister's boyfriends built the house and needed to find a buyer fast. I recall the sales price was around $13,000. It was a 3-bedroom, 2-bath (2000 sf) house at the end of a cul-de-sac and within a few blocks of the In-N-Out burger stand on Francisquito Ave next to the I-10 Freeway. At that time there were only two In-N-Out Burgers in existence. The other was on Ramona Boulevard very close to Baldwin Park High School. I later got a job there that lasted just a few months, but it was quite an experience. The place was always busy as the kids with their shiny hot rods and fancy cars would continually frequent the place, sometimes 2 or 3 times a night, always with their radios blaring out the latest rock n' roll sounds. It was the real life version of American Graffiti. (Big Girls Don't Cry – The Four Seasons)

My senior year in high school was pretty special in many ways, no more job, no sports of any kind, but not much freedom. For my last year I elected to take an electronics class as I heard that the students got to make crystal sets (radios). However, during my first day in class, the instructor, Mr. Larry Wolfe, told the students that he had a special project he wanted us to tackle the upcoming year. There would be no "crystal sets" made this year. There were only eight students in the class. Mr. Wolfe explained that he had reviewed the transcripts of everyone who wanted to take his electronics class had personally selected the students who were present, excluding all others.

Of all the instructors I've had in school at any level, Mr. Wolfe left the greatest impression on me by far. Many of the other students in our class would probably say the same thing. He was an instructor, a mentor, a motivator, and when all was said and done, he was a friend. Ron Sinnen, John Arvizu, Steve Schaefer, Steven King, Ron Dyste, Noel Leckness and I attended that class. All were incredibly intelligent kids.

> Ron Sinnen had a 200 I.Q., scored a perfect 1600 on the SAT and worked at JPL in Pasadena in the space program.

> John Arvizu became a doctor and worked at Kaiser Permanente Hospital in San Francisco.

Noel Leckness became a college math professor and taught in his home state of Oklahoma.

I found out information about my classmates years later from Ron Sinnen's father, Lanny, who was a civil engineer, a bowler and a friend. After Ron graduated from high school, he attended Northrup Institute of Technology in Inglewood on a full scholarship (JPL's private Think Tank). Ron Dyste and Steven King both went to Berkeley for their university studies. Steve Schaefer was a jerk and I could care less what happened to him.

Mr. Wolfe laid out his project. He wanted to accomplish something that had never been done in any high school in America, or anywhere else that he knew. He wanted us to build a closed-circuit television system from a schematic. It would be a first if we succeeded (another first, huh?). The commitment we made to him was simple. No sports. No clubs. No outside activities. We were to be studying electronic theory in his classroom every morning <u>before</u> school started and, in addition, work on the project in the afternoons <u>after</u> our final period completed. I won't describe the tasks we accomplished as they were tedious and would not be very interesting. We were allowed to listen to music on the radio in the afternoons and a new craze was booming—surfing. Not only had the Beach Boys arrived, but a duo with a catchy sound was getting a lot of attention. Jan & Dean had a #1 hit that would become the nickname for the city of Hunting Beach and the surfing tournaments held there. The song was called "Surf City." (Surf City—Jan & Dean)

I remember buying a kit for $25 and building my own surfboard. My friend, Jimmie (who lived across the street), and I spent long hours mixing and applying fiberglass to our balsa wood boards. They didn't look very professional, that's for sure. But, they worked and we enjoyed 'catching' the waves on them at Huntington Beach or Malibu. The following year, when I felt pretty confident on my board, I was screaming across the face of a wave (always loved speed), but couldn't control the board. I bailed as the board went smashing into one of the pilings on the Huntington Beach pier, busting in half. I had other friends who surfed so I borrowed boards when I could. Surfing was fun, just a great experience.

When May 1963 rolled around, we fired up our new TV system. Obstacles and some set-backs are always anticipated, but we didn't have many at all. My specialty was coax cabling and that skill served me well in later years. Our newly constructed equipment looked crude (it was) and bulky. Amazingly, the thing worked!

We had our own little "candid camera" at Baldwin Park High School. Catching students completely unaware they were being watched was downright funny and entertaining. The only piece of equipment that we purchased for our new television system was the videocon tube for the camera; Mr. Wolfe footed the bill, although he said it came from his Physics budget. All the other parts of the system were cannibalized from other electronics: radios, televisions, transmitters and receivers that were either donated or given to us because we begged a lot. When we told local electronic merchants what we intended to accomplish, they just shook their heads and said, "Good luck." Luck had nothing to do with it.

Chapter 11: Graduation Day

June 13, 1963, was my high school graduation day. Now this may seem a bit unbelievable, but I had 72 cousins on my mom's side and I was the first one to graduate from high school. Later, I would become the first to graduate from a university. On graduation night at BPHS I had friends with me: Paul (my cousin) and his girlfriend, Diane Ehrbar, Paul Adamcik (best friend), and Charmaine. No one from my family attended, except for cousin, Paul. After the ceremonies, we headed to Bob's Big Boy in West Covina for a bite to eat. Later we drove to Burbank and the Pickwick Recreation Center for my senior party. It wasn't nearly as extravagant as the graduation parties these days, but we had stellar entertainment: Chuck Berry (Johnny B. Good). We spent most of our time ice-skating, shooting pool and goofing off. It was an enjoyable, fun evening. Just fun. No drinking, no drugs, no sex. Just clean fun. Our group enjoyed the party and had a great time. Would you believe that the #1 song in the country when I graduated was sung by a guy would didn't speak English? (Sukiaki—Kuy Sakamoto)

After high school, I had no idea what I was going to do in my life; I just wasn't prepared for anything. Aimlessly, I started college at Mt. San Antonio Junior College three times before I was drafted into the Army and dropped out three times.

While walking across the Mt. SAC campus on Friday morning, November 22, 1963, an announcement was broadcast that stopped me in my tracks. President John F. Kennedy had been assassinated in Dallas that morning. Like so many other Americans I was stunned and didn't know what the future would be like without our President. Kennedy was admired by everyone. At that time in my life I considered myself a liberal democrat as the ideals of the Democratic party paralleled mine, but I was young and had much to learn about politics and the self-serving interests of those in power. What I actually knew about politics and the trappings contained in its vicious circle would have covered about 3 pages in a comic book. Shortly thereafter, I dropped out of school again; I just couldn't afford to stay in school. Life sucked.

I got a job in Industry at a place called Cinch Graphics where I worked in the plating department. I was trained in the plating processes for copper, nickel, gold and platinum. My lead man (boss) would try to explain the conversion equations for the amount of electrical current to use in the individual plating tanks. He was usually frustrated with me as I would give him the answer before he could figure it out on paper, simple algebra was beyond him. I was paid $1.95 an hour and after a month I got a big raise to $2.10 an hour. What a waste, but I needed a job so I endured. Besides, my flunky job financed my gambling: pool, bowling and the horses. On the lighter side, I would gold plate nickels, dimes and quarters and silver plate pennies. Alicia has some of those coins as I gave them to her as a gift. On the downside, the chemicals in the plating tanks were replaced periodically, always on my shift in the middle of the night. To accomplish this, the tanks were emptied into cement channels where a caustic soda neutralizer had been dumped. The chemicals traveled in the cement channel, through the caustic soda and straight into the sewer system. Ouch ! ! !

During this time my dad was seeing a lot of Dolores and after a short while they were married and the family at home was now huge. I moved out. Like teenagers everywhere, Charmaine and I had occasional flare-ups that caused us to break up time and again, always to reunite. Life wasn't much fun. (Deep Purple—Nino Tempo & April Stevens)

After a few months one of the men I bowled with at La Puente Lanes named John DeVite got me a job where he worked in Covina. I was now making the big bucks, $2.75 an hour. I worked there for about a year before I was fired for busting a guy in the chops. I had quite a temper and I always seemed to be in dutch. I was 19 years old and getting dumber every day. I had no direction, no motivation, and no mentor; I desperately needed a hero. I existed, but that was about it. Don't get the wrong impression;

I wasn't depressed, just misdirected. There were plenty of fun times and I enjoyed life as much as any young person when I had the opportunities. What I lacked was direction, character and substance, but not much else.

1964 brought The Beatles to the U.S. and their music was mesmerizing. They busted on the scene with I Wanna Hold Your Hand and followed it with many, many #1 hits. The music in the sixties was the best ever. Rock was evolving and it came at you from all sides all at once. The Four Seasons, The Beatles, and Motown. The Motown sound developed mostly by Barry Gordy and Phil Specter in Detroit gave rise to young and talented performers like Smokey Robinson, Mary Wells, The Marvelettes, The Supremes (Diana Ross) and The Cookies. The latter group would be featured prominently in an Oscar Winning Best Picture titled "Ray" in 2005 about the life of Ray Charles. All the new sounds were fantastic and captured turbulent moments in our country's history, but all had to contend with The Beatles. In April 1964, the top five songs in the country were all Beatles songs: Can't Buy Me Love; Twist & Shout; She Loves You; I Wanna Hold Your Hand; and Please, Please Me. The Beatles held 14 spots on Billboard's Top 100, the greatest monopoly ever or since on the Top 100 by any artist or group. (I Saw Her Standing There – The Beatles)

I have few memories from 1964 and 1965 that are worth mentioning, except those with Charmaine. Oh, I enjoyed the music a great deal and I gambled to make ends meet, doing quite well at times and living in the dungeon at others. Peaks and valleys seemed the way life would treat me. I didn't work much in '65 as I was a student of horse racing and I went to the track nearly every day (Santa Anita, Hollywood Park, Los Alamitos or Del Mar). I studied the Daily Racing Form and could tell you just about every detail of handicapping.

In the evenings, I would travel around Los Angeles with a couple friends who were also pretty astute at Bowling. One friend in particular named "Bo" Behonik was one of the best around in those days, probably because he was a pill head always using speed. Bo and I would bowl doubles against just about anyone. At the time of the Watts Riots in 1965, Bo and I would frequent Luxor Bowl on Western Avenue which was smack dab in the middle of the black area of Los Angeles. We had an "in" to get into the place. A black guy named Luke Asbury bowled in a scratch league at Bowling Square in Pasadena. He was the only black bowler in the league and he was on my team! I find it interesting that in sports color doesn't matter a bit, only talent does. In any event, Luxor Bowl was burned down during the riots.

Charmaine and I enjoyed only a few "special dates" together, probably because we didn't have much money. I remember a special place though: the Teenage Fair in 1964 (Hollywood Palladium). At the Teenage Fair we saw Sonny & Cher and danced to the music of The Challengers (Surfbeat). Other than that, we mostly went to the movies or hung out at Bob's Big Boy in West Covina, In 'n Out Burger in Baldwin Park, or the A&W Root Beer hang out on Whittier Boulevard in Whittier. Besides spending weekends roller skating in Baldwin Park or ice skating in West Covina, we'd go to the beach with friends or to a party, nothing very special though. I have searched my mind over and over about her and I have come to understand that my feelings for her (and hers for me) were probably mutually dependent and not very deep at all. How could they be? We were very young and lacking in maturity even though we would never admit that. It was a tough time for us both and we clung to each other for the support we didn't get at home, and I did love her. (I Get Around—Beach Boys)

Age 17

Chapter 12: Drafted into Johnson's War

Towards the end of December 1965, I received an extraordinary invitation in the mail. It was from my Uncle Sam. I was invited, at no cost to me, to join the U.S. Army as a draftee where I would receive free hair-cuts, room & board, clothes, and weapons training. I could hardly wait! (Don't you dare believe that!) On the morning of April 21, 1966, Charmaine drove me to the draft board in downtown Los Angeles. It was the beginning of my Army career and the beginning of the end of my relationship with her. Our goodbye wasn't all that warm, sort of like 'see ya' and then we parted. It was as if we were just acquaintances. She went her own way as I was whisked away to El Paso, Texas, for basic training. The person I missed most when I went into the service was my little step-sister, Vanessa. She was so playful and always full of life. Before I left, I held her on my knee and told her I would be back someday and we would play again, and she gave me a big hug. Some things you never forget. (The Sound Of Silence—Simon & Garfunkel)

Up to that point in time, I was a "never was." You see, if you were a 'never was' you couldn't be accused of being a 'has been.' My life was in limbo and I was just stagnant, doing the same thing tomorrow that I did the day before. Going into the service at that time in my life was absolutely the best thing that could have happened to me. I was young, arrogant, obnoxious, and many times a complete jerk. Oh, I had my moments where I was charming, flattering and as pure as the driven snow, but those moments were far less numerous than my tantrums. I was a disaster waiting to find a place to happen. Charmaine and I had many difficulties resulting from my insane jealousy and to be honest, I don't know why she put up with it. I would make a turn about in the service, but that day was down the line and I wouldn't see it coming anyway. (Summertime—Billy Stewart)

Here I was, 21 years old and basically uneducated, except for my street sense. Sure, I was intelligent and quick-witted, but for the most part I had no direction. I oozed confidence and self-esteem, but it was just a smoke screen. I was a loser, but here is a very solid, personal and enlightening observation: I knew it! Uncle Sam would soon take care of that point. The only thing I really knew how to do well was gamble and I had provided for my existence by gambling for the past few years. Besides bowling, I was a pool shark and card player. My best game at pool was golf, played on a snooker table. It required a great deal of patience and strategy. The most important element was patience and I had loads of that, especially when there were funds to be made. I did quite well gambling at cards as I had an uncanny ability to read people. There were more 300 games in competition, and I won a few local bowling tournaments and had developed a reputation as a hustler. I was pretty good at just about everything that meant nothing.

In my first four months in the Army I learned, the hard way most of the time, to respect authority. Although it was a painfully slow process, my life was making a subtly positive change and that was a good thing. For basic training, I was stationed in the desert at Fort Bliss in El Paso, Texas, for eight miserably hot, tortuous weeks. It would get so hot during the day that the red ants wouldn't come out. On one of our forced marches in BT, we were to march 6 miles into the desert and 6 miles back. Just before we left, the D.I.s (drill instructors) had us empty our canteens; it was over 100 degrees out there. More than 20 soldiers ended up in the infirmary from heat stroke. Life wasn't fair at all, or so it seemed, and it was getting worse.

I was a young gun still oblivious to the world and still defiant. That was changing as I discovered the Army isn't fair either. A great deal of physical effort is expended in boot camp and near the end there is a PT (Physical Training) Test for the recruits consisting of five events. 100 points possible for each event. You'll have to forgive me, because I don't remember all the events (I'm old). I do remember the horizontal rings; an obstacle course; throwing live grenades; and the mile run in full combat gear. The highest score ever recorded in my company was 465 out of 500 points. If you could beat that score you would be given a weekend pass into El Paso. The most difficult task was the mile run. To get 100 points there, you had to run the mile under 6 minutes. Piece of cake. I scored 485 points—new record! Did I get my weekend pass? No. Of course not. My score was ignored. Seems the D.I.s didn't take kindly to my gambling habits or my attitude. Oh, well. While waiting for the bus to take us to the airport for our first 'leave' home, I hustled the others pitching quarters; made about $50 as I recall.

After basic training, I was sent to Fort Jackson in South Carolina for A.I.T. (Advanced Infantry Training). I was in the Army during Johnson's War or so it was called because President Lyndon Johnson escalated the conflict in Viet Nam. It was no secret that most of the kids drafted were going "over the pond" to fight in Southeast Asia. While stationed at Fort Jackson, I was volunteered (several times) by the sergeants to perform Kitchen Police or KP (wouldn't have happened if I had kept my mouth shut). I was still spouting off at the wrong time to the wrong person. One evening after dinner when I had finished cleaning the pots and pans and we were ready to leave, the mess sergeant had me take supplies from the mess hall to his car. Thought that was strange so I tested him.

As I was leaving the mess hall, I was carrying a rack of ribs left over from dinner back to the barracks. The mess sergeant asked me what I thought I was doing. I politely said the ribs were not going to his car. He didn't utter a word. My buddies and I enjoyed another tasty dining experience.

Near the end of training, there was another PT Test. Fort Jackson was a lot nicer and a whole lot prettier than Ft. Bliss and the competition was just as much fun (I loved competing in anything). Again, I scored tops in my company. What fun. Did I get my weekend pass? You figure it out. The mess sergeant had friends.

Following A.I.T. in July 1966, I received orders sending me to some obscure place in Viet Nam. I had three weeks before I left so I was assigned temporarily to the Reception Center at Fort Jackson, with nothing to do. My first Saturday there, I wandered into the bowling center at Fort Jackson. That day changed my future and quite possibly saved my life. There was a pot game going on for a buck a head so I asked if I could participate.

The guys chuckled and someone said another sucker was always welcome, especially one with no hair. I didn't take kindly to that comment.

I remember that Saturday as clearly as any in my life. I put on a pair of rented bowling shoes and grabbed a ball off the rack that seemed to fit my hand and started to practice. I hadn't bowled in four months so I was a little rusty, but soon regained my stride. There were probably a dozen or so guys in the game. None of them were recruits and none of them were very good either. They were all soldiers stationed at Fort Jackson. The first game I bowled 209 and won! I won the next game, too, and most of the guys quit saying I was too lucky. One of the bowlers, named Bill, stayed and we bowled heads-up. Jokingly, I asked him how much he could afford to lose. He said he would bowl me for $10. Rudely, no, sarcastically, I told him I wouldn't put my shoes on for $10. He said I was a cocky kid and he wanted to know why. Imagine that, someone wanted to "know" me, that was different. So I told him I was going to Viet Nam in three weeks and nothing much mattered to me. We bowled two games, total score, for $25 and I stomped him.

It was easy to see that Bill was a competitive guy, even though he was pretty old, about 50 I'd say. He said he 'liked competition' and was interested in bowling me heads-up again, perhaps next week, but not anymore this day. Although he said I was probably better than him, he enjoyed the challenge. (Probably???) So I told him he could lose today or he could lose next week, it didn't matter. He gave me the strangest look as he left.

During the following week I went into Columbia (the capitol) and bought a new bowling ball and started practicing. I bowled every day for hours. I was on temporary duty and had nothing else to do so I practiced and practiced. My competitive game came roaring back. In the evenings I would spend time at the post library listening to Buddy Holly albums and feeling forlorn. Here I was in the south, not that South Carolina wasn't a beautiful place, it was, waiting to be sent thousands of miles away to fight in a stupid war in a foreign country I had no reason to believe was going to benefit anyone. I was going to the jungle, for Christ's sake. The thing that concerned me most was that I had no control over anything, not even my own life. In my lonely moments, and there were plenty of those, I thought about Charmaine. What a waste. She certainly wasn't thinking of me. Buddy Holly became my best friend. (Crying, Waiting, Hoping—Buddy Holly)

Bill and I went at it again the following Saturday. This time the ante went up. We bowled three games, total score for the three games, for $100. The place was packed as if everyone on post had heard about the match game or so it seemed. $100 was all the cash I could muster at the time, but Bill didn't know that. Out of the chute, I slammed 279 at him. The place was buzzing. As it turned out, Bill quit half way through the final game. He said I had beaten him fair and square and although he had lost, he enjoyed the competition. I couldn't believe this guy. I had just crushed him competitively and he was being nice about it. He was gracious and polite. On the other hand, I was not. I was still a little steamed at being called a sucker the previous week by some bozo who didn't possess enough talent to carry my bowling bag. With a wryful smile, I asked Bill if he would like to get his money back and he just held up his arm like a stop sign. He shook his head slowly. Softly and graciously he said, "No, sir. I can't beat you."

That statement stopped me cold. He was pleasant and friendly and so we chatted for a few minutes. He wanted to know how long I had been bowling. "Since I was 14," I told him. For some reason I liked Bill. Maybe because he was older or perhaps it was because of his warm, charismatic manner. Hmmm, charisma. That was probably it. Additionally, he treated me with respect and not with the disgust I had been enduring the previous four months of Army captivity. Then I had a thoughtful insight: people respond to how you treat them, just as I was doing. Interesting, indeed. Out of that conversation came a moment of weakness or, perhaps, something touched me deep inside and so, for a few moments, I took my defensive barrier down and grudgingly told him he was right. He couldn't beat me. Then I did something completely out of character and foreign to my then personality. I took his $100 off the table, rolled it up, reached over and stuck it in his shirt pocket and said, "You didn't have a chance." He looked shocked and asked me what I thought I was doing. He said it was a fair match. "No, it wasn't," I straightforwardly told him. I apologized for taking advantage of him and the others and further explained that I had bowled professionally when drafted and I had made my living bowling prior to being drafted into the Army, and that losing never entered my mind. That's what made it so easy.

He eyed me for a few moments and then asked, "How would you like to work for me, Steve?" I had no idea what he meant so I reminded him I was heading off to Viet Nam in a couple weeks, but what the heck, I could use a job making a few extra bucks before I left. He mentioned he was aware of that fact and he asked me if I knew where Owen's Field was. I said I did (I really didn't) and he said to come see him first thing Monday morning, in uniform, of course. Later that evening in the post library, Buddy Holly and I were relaxing together and I thought to myself, "Steven, you're an idiot." I was just terribly alone with no control in my life.—I was the "nowhere man." (Nowhere Man—The Beatles)

I didn't know where Owen's Field was located even though I told Bill I did, but I learned it was an Army Air-Base. It wasn't difficult to find and when I arrived, I noticed there were no airplanes, just helicopters. The 3rd Army Helicopter Headquarters was at Owen's Field. Just as Bill told me, I was there bright and early, about 11:30 in the morning. Time meant little to me as I was heading overseas shortly and I slept late while I could. Oh, I wasn't in uniform either. Besides, I didn't know what Bill did for a living. Boy! Was I in for a rude awakening.

When I entered the headquarters building and asked for Bill, I got the shock of my life. I was given some very peculiar looks from the officers there. A lieutenant and a captain asked me, individually, why I wanted to see Bill. Shortly thereafter I was ushered into the C.O.'s (Commanding Officer) office. Behind a large, shiny oak desk was Bill Hundley, Colonel Bill Hundley (sic). I uttered, "Oh, shit." He was in charge of 3rd Army Aviation at Fort Jackson, responsible for recruitment of Warrant Officers to fly combat helicopters in Viet Nam. He looked up at one stunned soldier boy, smiled and said, "I'm going to ask you one more time. Do you want to work for me?" I silently nodded in the affirmative and he asked me for a copy of my written orders sending me to Viet Nam. Fortunately, I had a copy with me. He handed the copy to the captain without looking at it and told him, "Take care of this." He told me to have a seat.

The Colonel asked me what my rank was. In the military your pay grade or rank is designated E-1 to E-9 for non-commissioner officers. I told him I was an E-1, the lowest rank in the Army. What I actually said was," The only thing lower than me is whale shit on the bottom of the ocean." He said, "Not any more. You're an E-3 (PFC) as of today. I like you, Steve, and I find your personality refreshing, but the chip has to go. Understand. It was not a question as his look said it all. Get your stripes and report back here tomorrow at 07:00. Is that understood, private?" I was promoted to PFC (private first class, E-3). Wow! Couldn't believe my blind luck. "Oh, one more thing," he said. "Get rid of the bowling ball. You won't have time for it anymore." Payback!

When I arrived Monday morning, Bill called me in for a chat. He was brutally honest, and yet soft-pedaled the conversation (he was the teacher, I was his student). As a military lifer, he had a marvelous personality with the ability to 'see' right through someone. He told me very plainly that he knew I was scared and that it wasn't uncommon. In fact, he said it was all too common. He also said that he asked me to work for him because I outwardly showed a great deal of fire. He respected that and said it would be beneficial to me if, somehow, I learned how to corral it. My emotions melted away. I still don't know how he did it, but he stripped me bare on the spot. Right then I knew I would do anything for this guy. Bill Hundley (I'm not sure of the spelling) and his staff were very positive influences on me and I grew to respect them for it. Once again that's not right either, not the right word. That's not what I mean. It was more than just respect; I was grateful for it. I was maturing (thanks to the Army) and didn't even realize it. That's not correct either. I was starting to build character and it would take a very long time to develop, but that was the genesis of the person I am today. I will never forget that man. The puzzle was coming together.

Off-site housing was out of the question with my miserable income so I was to remain permanently housed at the reception center in the barracks. As it turned out, all the new recruits came through the reception center and part of my job was to greet them early on. And I had a private room! Wow!

My very unusual, out of character, kind-hearted gesture of giving him back his $100 on Saturday afternoon turned out to truly be a blessing in disguise. (Don't you love the use of the split-infinitive!) No longer was I headed to Viet Nam to fight in Johnson's war. I had been in the Army for four months and gotten exactly nowhere with anyone, except that my M.O.S. (Military Occupational Specialty) was 11B40 which is Army lingo for Light Infantry, Automatic Weapons. In other words, I was a foot soldier who would carry an M-16 into combat and march through the jungles of Viet Nam. However, my luck had changed and my new M.O.S. was 91H20 or "Personnel Specialist." That's really funny as I didn't know how to type. I was given a gift that was precipitated by an act of honesty and kindness on my part. I was learning fast and I felt a sense of pride growing inside of me. What's more, I got a permanent home, the Reception Center at Fort Jackson. It wasn't much, but it was permanent. That was my first Army blessing. The best was yet to come.

Chapter 13: Susie Darlin'

My job in the Army for the next 20 months would be to screen recruits at the Reception Center in the mornings and administer the written flight test to them and to military pilots from the Army, Navy, Air-Force, Marines and Coast Guard in the evenings. Those who wanted to receive rotary-wing training to become helicopter pilots and who were fortunate enough to get through the program had to extend for an additional year in the service, but that was a cheap price to pay for flight training worth more than a million bucks. I would have given it a "go" but for my bad right eye and lack of a college degree. In order for me to perform my assignment, I had to know what I was talking about so I studied the exams and asked lots of questions from the lieutenant and captain who conducted the initial orientations. I learned quickly.

My rank improved as a consequence. Six months later, after I had been in the service for 10 months, I was a Specialist E-5 or Spec-5 (bird sergeant) as was commonly the term. As a draftee, E-5 was as high a grade as you could attain in two years. It was the same rank as sergeant, except I specialized in one particular area. Life was good and I actually enjoyed my service time from then on, but for a far different reason.

Well, I was settling in at the reception center when the blind side came. I received the letter that so many of my friends had received, the Dear John letter. Charmaine had found someone else and was permanently out of my life. "Now what?" I thought. Life went on. Charmaine and I were always bickering about something, mostly because she wanted to date other guys. I could sense when speaking with her on the phone that she was "distant" from me as I must have also sounded to her. As the weeks went by, it seemed the only time I missed her was when I was alone and lonely (most of the time).

As the days passed I was learning my way around the reception center area where I was to work and sleep. And then it happened. It wasn't expected and I wasn't looking for it. It just happened. I met Susan.

One morning in the mess hall, I walked by a table with this very attractive WAC sitting there by herself. She had a Specialist-5 ranking (I was a PFC) so I thought better of speaking to her at that point. Jesus! A Spec-5, she was important! I made a promise to myself to learn more about her. I learned or was told that she was engaged to some guy in Louisiana. Honestly, I didn't know if that was true or not and it didn't matter anyway. What I did know was that he was there and she was here. Bad luck for him.
(Susie Darlin'—Robin Luke)

This is all coincidence that I first mention Susie in chapter 13. She was born on the 13th (January) as I was (March).

Chapter 14: A Perfect Love?

If either of you believes I can describe or define love in any way, you have obviously been drinking too much of your own bath water. Your dad is just a simple man, no better than any other, but certainly different. And so I will just describe how I felt in the simplest terms available to me when I first met Susan. J*DJ N#&D D_RF#&FD. There, how does that sound?

After a couple days of inquiring about this young beauty, I decided that it was now or never. At breakfast one morning, she was sitting in the same seat at the same table as before when I approached her. She looked up smiling and I asked if I could join her. I would have been crushed if she had said no, but she didn't. I felt like I was 16 again. We struck up a friendly conversation and I was falling all over myself. The same old unfamiliar feeling of being socially ignorant was still with me, causing me to fumble like a fool. As usual, I did a pretty good doing just that. We gazed at each other and talked for the longest time and I have absolutely no idea what we said.

After that morning, we met for meals often, and over the next few days I couldn't wait to see her, talk to her, look at her. She consumed me in silence. After a week or so, maybe longer, I don't remember, I asked her if she liked to play cards. That was really smart, wasn't it? How dumb of me. Here I was, Mr. Arrogant, and I was stumbling all over the place. She said, "Sure." We planned on an afternoon get together at 2:00 p.m. on the grass.

Later than afternoon Susan and I played cards (gin rummy) and made small talk over who knows what. To this day, I still have no idea what we talked about. All I could see was her and she was magnetic. What I do remember, quite vividly, is at the moment of perfection, I pulled her close and kissed her. Amazingly, she kissed me back, tenderly and with a very warm and enchanted feeling. Wow ! ! ! I was breathless and my heart was pounding uncontrollably and I tried not to let it show. When I looked in her eyes, she sparkled and I felt an emotion that would last a lifetime.

Often in solitude I think back on that day with tenderness and I smile. She was the one; I felt it and I knew it. How on Earth and why did God drop this angel on me? Given a little time and effort, I was to unravel a perfect beginning. But I can say one thing for certain here. Loving her was the easiest thing I ever did. (Sunny—Bobby Hebb)

To that point in my life, I had had exactly one girlfriend: Charmaine. I thought that's how it was supposed to be. I didn't realize that the one you love sometimes doesn't love you back with the same intensity. Sometimes they don't really love you at all. Besides, I was a tenderfoot, a rookie. I knew nothing about love and relationships; I never had the opportunity to learn. Even if I had, it still doesn't mean I couldn't screw it up.

Over time your dad has learned a great deal about life and mellowed because of it. Everyone has their own concepts of love that seem to be right (for them, anyway), but for me, I'll just explain with music this way:

> "You can't see it with your eyes, or hold it in your hands,
> But like the wind that covers our land,
> Strong enough to rule the heart of any man, this thing called love
>
> It can lift you up, never let you down,
> Take your world and turn it all around,
> Ever since time nothing's ever been found that's stronger than love"
>
> . . . Johnny Cash

It's difficult to explain how emotions work so I'll just say that I never "feel" love as much as I experience it. You can love someone and not like them, or you can think you love someone and for some reason it doesn't work. But you'll never know unless you go for it. I have fallen into and out of love so many times it's staggering, thanks to Buscaglia (you'll learn about him later). It's not difficult as I wear my emotions on my sleeve and I always remain vulnerable, and I do it purposely. No more barriers. If it works it works, and that's terrific. But if it doesn't, don't stagnate your life with misery and loneliness. I refuse to be the man Henry David Thoreau described when he wrote, "Most men lead lives of quiet desperation and go to the grave with the song still in them." Every time I have fallen for someone, and I mean every time, something has been missing, except with Susan. The depth of emotion I grew with her was warm, encompassing, and fulfilling. Everything was there and in place. Everything. I truly felt privileged just to be in her company. And like the fool I am, I let it slip away and I have paid dearly for that mistake my entire life. I'll restate my feelings by saying, "Susan was the light in my life and I have lived in the shadows since 1968."

Susie and I had a great deal in common, or at least I believed we did. We liked the same things, same music, and the same movies. Most of all, we liked each other's company. There was only one thing about Susan that I wondered about. She never spoke of her past or where she came from. Me? I couldn't talk enough. I was the original motor-mouth. The only thing I knew about her was that she came from Monroeville, Ohio, wherever that was.

Everything I mention about Susan is joyful and I have no memory of any quarrels or disputes, although there were probably a few. I just don't remember. What I remember most about her is the "million dollar smile." Whenever I think of her, I melt.

Just before Christmas 1967 Susie went home on leave and when she returned she seemed distant. I don't know why, but that bothered me a great deal. I had never felt that feeling before and it scared me. Although she was quiet and reserved, I thought she would tell me. She never did. I never asked.

On my E.T.S. (End of Term of Service) in April 1968, I headed back to California driving a new 1968 Dodge Charger. Susie was with me. The #1 song in the country was a beautiful country ballad, Honey (Bobby Goldsboro), but the song that really caught my fancy was Do You Know

The Way To San Jose (Dionne Warwick), because I was driving across the country from South Carolina to California.

There had always been a lot of down time in the service and I had made up my mind that Steven, the 'never was', would be no longer. Steven would acquire a college degree and make something of his pointless life. During my Army career I had seen all sides: the poor, the ignorant, the educated, and those born with the golden horseshoe. Surveying my background and family history, I steadfastly refused to stay in limbo and I would make something of my life. There was only one university I would attend: UCLA. There would be no other. One benefit from being in the service was the G.I. Bill, although it is far different today than when I was in the service. I would be given two months of college eligibility for each month of service commitment. Uncle Sam was going to send me to school for 4 years.

Susie and I traveled leisurely across the country and I sensed a stressful situation developing that I just couldn't handle. When we arrived in the bay area where Susie was to live, I was silent (as usual) and troubled as if everything was coming down and I'm sure she felt the same way. Her words, when I left, haunt me still. "Don't leave me . . . ," was all I remember.

Well, I left and although she has forgiven me, I have never forgiven myself. I loved her deeply and I left. It was absolutely true. Steven was an idiot. Although I didn't know it then, I would carry this burden of guilt with me my entire life, and I would carry it alone. I had left the love of my life and would be destined to be the master of the rebound romance, constantly searching for the perfect love and knowing all too well it had slipped through my fingers. There would be many more mistakes made in my life, but none would ever top this one.

Over the years I have been in company where prayers or blessings of all types have been offered for a myriad of occasions, some very touching and heartfelt. No one has ever heard a word from my mouth. I won't participate even though I have been invited several times. I can't and I won't. All requests have been met in silence and I simply will not participate because I carry an insurmountable burden with me, that I am not worthy. I should never have left her . . .

Chapter 15: My Best Friend Is Gone

After returning to California and taking some much needed time off, I started bowling again. Hustling again. Of course, I had to make a living the only way I knew how, but it wasn't easy and it wasn't without risks. What I mean is that bowling a guy for $20 when you only have $5 in your pocket can be a little perplexing. To "spot" my gambling, I collected unemployment for a few months and didn't look for work, for a short period anyway. Besides, how many employers were looking for "soldiers?"

After sitting on my duff for a few months and gambling just to exist, I obtained employment at Baldwin Park Bowl where I reestablished friendships I had left behind two years before, except for Charmaine. She and I were no longer close, but we remained friends and would talk periodically about the past, the present and the future. Paul Adamcik was still my best friend and we renewed our friendship and drank beer together, lots of beer. After all, it was the nectar of the Gods. We really liked beer so we made it a point to drink a great deal of it. Paul was a superb pool player; better than me most of the time and I was no slouch. We were very competitive, but in a good way. In all the years we knew each other, I don't recall Paul and me ever having an argument. The simple fact is we had our share of moments, lots of moments.

One day while we were riding in his grandmother's little green Nash Rambler (one of the ugliest cars ever invented, I might add), the right front wheel came completely off, tire, rim & hub, and rolled off to the right some place. We spun around and ground to a halt as the axle dug into the asphalt. When we got out of the car, people were just looking and laughing. There we were in the middle of Baldwin Park with a little Nash Rambler having only three wheels. A couple of guys we knew came running up and together, the four of us "picked up" the car and moved it to the curb. It was a hilarious moment that we joked about for hours, and we celebrated it with a few more beers. It was comical. I hated that car; it was really ugly, capital "U." (Beep Beep—Playmates)

During that summer in 1968, Paul and I made several trips to the beach blasting out Born To Be Wild (Steppenwolf) on my stereo. I had a flashy (and fast) new Dodge Charger and we were always getting the "stares" from the bikinis. The Charger was now equipped with a shiny set of chrome reverse wheels and looked super sharp. It was metallic blue and I had a pearlescent white stripe painted the length of the car over the driver's side. Life was fun and frenzied. We were two buddies out having fun and having a great time enjoying whatever we did, and it was all perfectly innocent. Just good, clean fun. Paul and I goofed off all summer and we were always playing jokes on one another. We were a couple of guys who were much too care free to take anything too seriously; I guess you could say we were too busy enjoying life and living in the moment. Paul's moments, however, were getting shorter and mine would somehow always drift away to the north.

As the summer progressed, Paul did something I had never thought of doing. He opened a checking account and put $25 in it. It's amazing how far $25 could go. I mean, he wrote checks everywhere and was always scrambling around or hustling pool to get the money to the bank. I told him it was silly, but one day while cruising around, I ran out of gas. No problem, Paul wrote a check. Life was good. And then, unexpectedly, it happened again.

One summer evening after enjoying a night of playing pool at Baldwin Park Bowl, I dropped Paul off at home around 2:00 o'clock in the morning. It was the last time I would ever see him. On his way up the stairs, Paul had a heart attack and died where his grandparents found him in the morning. Paul Adamcik was just 22 years old. Another sad moment and another death to someone close to me, but there was little grieving this time. Paul and I had talked about death many times and thought of it not as an end but as a challenge, much like Don Quixote. Somehow Paul knew his time on Earth would not be a long one and he lived it that way.

Paul (on right)

He and I had made a pact that if either one of us left early in life, the other would celebrate, not the death, but the life. He and I believed in living every day to its fullest. My best friend received a tremendous send-off celebration. On the evening of his funeral, I kept my promise and fulfilled our pact. Several of his friends, including myself, held a going-away party at Baldwin Park Bowl where we closed the bar that night; the fun and dancing continued until dawn. It was daylight when we wrapped it up. Just before we left, we all raised our glasses and gave Paul a final toast. He was the best friend I would ever have. I missed my buddy and his quirky manner, but I gave him a super send-off. There are moments in solitude where, on reflection, I miss him still. Fair or unfair, life was moving on . . . .

Chapter 16: Back To School (UCLA)

Later that fall, while sitting in the bar at Eastland Lanes in West Covina, I lost another friend, one whom I had never had the pleasure of meeting. Judy In Disguise (John Fred) was playing on the jukebox when someone unplugged it and turned on the television news. Robert Kennedy had just been assassinated in Los Angeles by a rag-head.

I had completed and submitted my application to UCLA and anticipated an early answer. Although I had the grades to get in, the answer was not as forthcoming as I had anticipated., but by 1969, though, I was in class. Wow! What a school. UCLA spreads on large grounds, more than 400 acres and has around 35,000 students. A stroll under the large ficus trees gives you a sense of serenity and calm.

UCLA

I have many fond memories of my years as a Bruin. Initially, the classes were not what I thought they would be. You had to show up for the first day of class for sure, but after that you didn't have to attend any more, just show up and take the final exam. That, however, would be a really stupid thing to do. By far the most enjoyable classes I took were the two quarters on the "History of Jazz." Our instructor, Professor Charles Tanner (sic), had played alto trombone for the Glenn Miller Orchestra. His knowledge and story-telling ability left a deep and profound impression on me, especially the stories on the origins of jazz. I had always loved music as I grew up on country and pop, but this jazz was really something and could easily touch your soul. Melodies could bring tears to your eyes without any words. The more of jazz I learned, the more open my appreciation of music became, for all types of music, except Rap. Rap is crap. Period. (A Closer Walk—Pete Fountain)

In early 1972 the top song in America was American Pie (Don McLean) and one morning while waiting for our History of Jazz class to start I was playing it on my cassette recorder/player. Our class was held in Royce Hall in order to accommodate the more than 600 students in the class, and the sound of American Pie filled the auditorium. I turned it off as Professor Tanner took the stage. He announced to the class, "That's not jazz," and everyone laughed. "But it is very poetic and very beautiful. It's quite a song," he went on to say. The song was a poetic description of the day the music died when Buddy Holly and the Big Bopper were killed in a plane crash in an Iowa corn field in February, 1959.

Now don't laugh, but your dear old dad took a bowling class at UCLA for ½ a credit. To get an "A" in that class you had to average 175. I barely made it as I averaged a mere 218. The instructor actually had me assisting the other students in the class; I was a celebrity. Twice I was approached to join the UCLA bowling team. Not a chance I told them; I was already classified as a professional.

A fond memory comes to mind as I remember standing in line to buy season tickets for the coming basketball season. A few classmates of mine and me took turns waiting and joking in line for two days to buy tickets. It was cold outside so the university staff allowed the students to spend the nights in Pauley Pavilion. At 8:00 a.m. each day we were ushered outside, but we were warm at night. Basketball tickets at UCLA were "gold" and very, very difficult to get. When my turn came, I bought two season ticket books; the maximum for a student was two books. Having two books meant you could take almost any girl to the game and I used my tickets to my fullest advantage. The cost of a season ticket book (16 games) was $4 for students. That equates to 25¢ a game for each of the 16 games, what a bargain. I spent all of $8 (and 2 sleepless nights).

The 1973 NCAA Men's Division I Basketball Tournament involved 25 schools playing in single-elimination play to determine the national champion. It began on March 10, 1973, and ended with the championship game on March 26 in St. Louis, Missouri. A total of 29 games were played, including a third place game in each region and a national third place game. UCLA, coached by John Wooden, won the national title with a 87–66 victory in the final game over Memphis State, coached by Gene Bartow. This gave UCLA their 7th consecutive title. Bill Walton of UCLA was named the tournament's Most Outstanding Player. That year's Final Four marked the first time the championship game was televised on a Monday night in prime time, a practice which continues today.

Undoubtedly, UCLA is the most dominant basketball team in collegiate history. While I attended UCLA over a three-year period, the Bruins were in the midst of 10 national titles in a 12-year period, winning 7 in a row at one point. Had it not been for an upset loss the North Carolina State in the semi-finals in 1974, the streak would have been 9 straight. Chris probably knows this, but Alicia wouldn't. On second thought, Chris doesn't know as much as he thinks.

Graduating from UCLA was a difficult and daunting achievement, but a very rewarding adventure. I put little emphasis on grades in college not because mine were just so-so, but because there are so many factors affecting grades. I'll explain. Being a couple years older than most students, I was not nearly as naive as many of those in my classes, but received lower grades. Why? The answer is simple (to me anyway). Most students went to class, studied, prepared their assignments and performed fairly well. That was the expectation anyway. The majority of the student body at UCLA came from solid family backgrounds that provided the support that struggling students need to get through the process. My situation was a bit more complicated. There was no family support to rely on and I worked 50 hours a week (night shift) at different bowling centers while attending classes at UCLA full-time. With little sleep and a demanding schedule, my grades suffered, but I got through it okay. All in all, my collegiate experience was stimulating and enjoyable. It was an absolute pleasure attending UCLA and my life would be much better for having done it . . .

Chapter 17: Fabled Alice

Bowling had been a large part of my life since I was 14 years old, both competing and working. I'd always had a friendly manner about me and I was an asset to the owners of any establishment where I worked. Initially, I had worked in the coffee shop washing dishes, then I graduated to porter where I would clean bathrooms, mop floors and empty ashtrays. Later I learned how to work on the machines and was employed as a B–mechanic (pin-chaser) for a year. Even though there was a great deal of noise, it gave me time to study since I was in the back of the bowling center. A short while later, I graduated to working behind the desk doing all the associated chores. A friend of mine named Herb White came up to the desk one evening beaming a broad, infectious smile. He said, "Steve, I have something for you. I just bought a yearling filly and she's now in training at Santa Anita. Now pay attention and remember this: The first time she runs, at any race track, she's going to win. Her name is Fabled Alice. Remember that." Herb was quite a character and told jokes better than most stand-up comics. He owned Great Western Trucking and bowled in several leagues, although he wasn't very proficient at it.

It was during my junior year at UCLA that I nearly destroyed myself, and I gave it a good try, too. After feeling worn down and tired with a continual sinus cold that just wouldn't go away, I entered the UCLA Medical Center (medical is covered with tuition) complaining that I was having dry convulsions.

After several tests, one of the doctors told me that he had thoroughly read the x-rays of my head, but found nothing. I jokingly said, "Thanks a lot," and got a chuckle from him. He was serious, though, and told me that my body was reacting to abuse. "Your body is worn out, Steve. Simply put, you can't work full-time and go to school full-time. Quit school or quit your job, you can't do both." An unpleasant decision had to be made, but I kept doing both, if only for a short time. Fate was about to step in and change my course in life once again.

It was toward the end of my junior year and things weren't going so well. I was still struggling with my sinus problem, but I had to work to keep things going. One April evening near the end of the Spring quarter at UCLA, while working at Beverly Bowl in Montebello, I was glancing through the Sports Section of the Los Angeles Times. As I browsed the race entries for the next day, I noticed something that caught my attention. Entered in the 1st race at Hollywood Park was a filly named "Fabled Alice." I thought, "Nah, this can't be right." A friend of mine had the Daily Racing Form for the next day so I asked to see it. Sure enough, in the 1st race was an unraced maiden filly named Fabled Alice. I looked at the name of the owners and it said Johnson & White. (Herb, you sly devil.)

An excited feeling fell over me as I recalled Herb White's promise. "The first time she races, she's going to win. Don't forget." I remembered what he had told me two years earlier. As luck would have it, I couldn't go to the track (Hollywood Park) the next day because of final exams at UCLA. To cover this predicament I asked a buddy named Fat Leo (that's what we called him) to place a bet for me.

Leo was enormous, probably close to 300 pounds with scruffy black hair and dark, horn-rimmed glasses that he squinted through. He was a mail carrier for the Post Office! Figure that one out. I gave Leo $20 and asked him to make a parlay from Fabled Alice in the 1st race to Emmamia in the 4th race. Since I had spent a few years at the track and studied racing, I actually possessed a great deal of knowledge about thoroughbreds, speed ratings and breeding. Fabled Alice was a "tip" that I acted on. Emmamia was a two-year old speed demon on the turf out of (sired by) New Policy. New Policy was a champion two-year-old colt who may have been one of the favorites to win the Kentucky Derby until he injured himself and never raced again, but he sired many stakes winning horses, almost entirely sprint champions. Anyway, with a parlay bet, if the first horse wins, all the winnings are then bet on the second horse. I called a bookie named Pat Pond and made the same bet (yeah, I was still a hustler and knew a couple bookies). I told everyone who would listen about my past conversation with Herb White and his yearling purchase. I was energized, but had finals the next morning.

After work I was alone with my thoughts as I drove home, and all I could think of on the way was Fabled Alice. Following a couple hours of sleep, I was up and off to school for a cram session and then the exams. In the afternoon I was thoroughly exhausted as I readied for my drive to Montebello to work that night. I had completely forgotten about the races at Hollywood Park that day. Around 7:30 that evening, as was his style, Leo came sauntering into Beverly Bowl. Following a few short conversations with friends, Leo made his way up to the desk where I asked him, "How'd she do."

Without blinking an eye he said, "She won! And she went off at 65-1." I was stunned! Fabled Alice paid $132.60 for a $2 win ticket. I had bet $20 on her. That's $1326.00 and Leo, because of my parlay, bet it all on another horse. I never would have done that if I was at the track. Stunned, I asked Leo about Emmamia, and he tossed a stack of $100 win tickets on the counter. Immediately I experienced an empty feeling that Emmamia had lost and all the money was down the drain. With a quizzical expression that strained for an answer, I looked at Leo and he said, "I don't know. I didn't stay."

Hollywood Park

What??? I was frantic. The race results had already been broadcast on the radio and the late edition of the paper was out with the early results (first 3 races), but Emmamia was in the 4th race. We stayed up all night drinking black coffee and swapping lies in the coffee shop until the L.A. Times was dropped off around 5:30 in the morning. Turning to the race results in the rear of the Sports Section, I stared at the results of the 4th race that made my spirits soar. Emmamia had won in a breeze by 6 lengths as the solid favorite. I made $2800 for my $20 bet. Same bet with Pat.

Fabled Alice went off at odds of 65-1 that day and went wire to wire (start to finish, the new term used at the tracks is now 'gate to wire'). Herb was right. Man was he right. Herb said Fabled Alice was going to win and she did. (Thanks, Herb, wherever you are.) Over the next two weeks, I made enough money on the horses that allowed me NOT to work my senior year at UCLA. My medical issue had been resolved and the future looked inviting. You may find the following account a bit on the unbelievable side, but it's as true and the sky is blue.

One of the guys I touted Fabled Alice on was a young Korean kid named Gary who hung around Beverly Bowl to pass the time. His family owned a trash collection business and he casually threw his money around. Well, Gary came into Beverly Bowl Saturday night and asked me to come out to the parking lot where he displayed a brand new Buick Riviera he bought from his winnings on Fabled Alice, then he handed me an envelope containing a $10 win ticket on Fabled Alice worth $663. Then he said he would repay me by taking me to the quarter horse races at Los Alamitos the following Monday. Not the immediate Monday, but the following Monday.

By arranging my work schedule so I could get that Monday off, I rode out to Los Alamitos with Gary and Fat Leo. Gary told me there was a horse in the 2nd that was absolutely "guaranteed" to win that night (sorry, don't remember the horse's name). What I do remember is that it was the #6 horse in the 2nd race. When I looked at the program (quarter horse programs are like miniature Daily Racing Forms and show past race results), I couldn't help but notice that this horse had beaten a total of 2 other horses in 10 races! "No way this horse can win," I muttered.

Gary said not to worry. Uncertain as I was, Gary talked me into betting $400 on this horse to win (remember he had given me $663). Our #6 horse had gone off at more than 100-1 each time it raced. Well, it was well over 100-1 as the horses approached the starting gate for a 350 or 400 yard sprint, can't really remember the distance. A horse's odds are displayed on the "tote board" as the betting continues up to post time. The #6 horse's odds were a "blinking 99" which means over 100-1.

As the horses were entering the gate, the odds on our #6 horse dropped to 50-1, then 20-1, then 10-1, and finally 9-2 when the race started. He was the #6 horse and the race was fixed! The #5 horse broke and veered left and the #7 horse broke and went right. All anyone could hear was a loud "Come on 6" from the crowd. The #6 horse went straight and won easily and paid $11.20 to win, which equated to $2240 in my pocket. The jockeys on the #5 and #7 horses were each suspended for life, never to ride again. My winnings amounted to a little over $8,000 for two weeks. Well, your dad is no dummy and understands the pitfalls of gambling all too well. Since that incredible gift that paid for my senior year at UCLA, I have not bet on a horse again. Not once. It would be more than 20 years before I would go to the races again, and only then because of a challenge . . .

Chapter 18: What's Your Name?

During my final year at UCLA, I attended classes wearing cut-offs and sweat shirts and I was usually bare-footed, and I lived at the beach in Venice. It was one of the most relaxing years of my life. For entertainment, I did a great deal of fishing and played basketball, lots of basketball. Caught a baby octopus once and brought it along the shoreline in a bucket to show the kids. Lots of fun! Because of my lifestyle, I was in exemplary physical condition and would remain so my entire life, at least until the accident. My senior year was the most enjoyable year of education I had experienced, and my grade point average in my major course of study, Economics, was 2.0, just barely enough to graduate. I had fulfilled all my major's requirements by my junior year (working 50 hours a week, no less). Because of my lucky streak where I didn't have to work my senior year, my grade point average as a senior was 3.85, not bad, huh? Made the Dean's list, too.

Shortly after I graduated in December 1972, I left for Florida with Jerry McLaughlin (Never-On-Time Tom's roommate), a bowling and poker-game buddy of mine who was to attend heavy equipment driving school in Homestead, Florida. I wasn't doing anything anyway, so off to Florida we went, just to be in the moment. While driving cross-country, we stopped to rest one evening in Selma, Alabama, where the civil rights marches had been held a few years earlier. That night, UCLA beat Memphis State for another basketball title. Bill Walton set an NCAA record by making 21 of 22 shots. Life was good. For the next few months I lived in North Miami Beach doing odd jobs and just kicking back. Many exploring adventures awaited me in the Everglades, as well as fishing and just goofing off. One day I was personally escorted from the Everglades by park rangers just because I was trying to catch a baby alligator. Obviously, they had no sense of humor. While relaxing and reflecting, I believe that trip to Florida was a superb way to unwind and recover from years of study and work, and I'd recommend it to anyone seeking to refresh his soul.

Rest and recuperating were things I needed, but surviving required real cash. When I did return to California later in 1973, I was broke and needed a job. I had made many friends while working at San Gabriel Lanes in San Gabriel and I renewed those friendships with zeal. My social life was open and free. During the summer, I would water ski and hang-glide; in the winter I followed the snow. There were instances where we would water ski on one weekend and snow ski the next. I went on ski vacations with my friends, both water and ski. During those enjoyable times, I had a girlfriend named Diane Stevens who was Miss San Gabriel in 1970. Diane was tall and curvy with long brown hair, nearly to her waist. She had beautiful blue eyes and a Marie Osmond smile. Yet again, there was something missing. She was a real looker, but on the downside, she was not intellectual at all, probably what many would consider an 'air-head.'

Over the years, sometimes through embarrassment, sometimes through experience, I've learned that looks are definitely not the best indicator on how a relationship will work. Always a slow learner in life it seemed, I was especially slow learning about women, a trait that continues to this day. And why not, I was usually concerned only with myself. The center of the universe was obviously me. Diane asked me one day why everyone always called me Steve when my birth name was Forrest. I really couldn't answer that question since I had always been called Steve, Stevie when I was a youngster. Diane joked about her last name and mine being almost identical so why shouldn't we get married. That was not in the cards. I had already been burned with Susan and was not interested, thank you very much. We talked about it, but she probably knew I wasn't interested in a deeper relationship.

At Diane's suggestion and since I had no close family ties, I changed my name from Forrest Clayton Steven, Jr., to Steven Forrest (no middle name, didn't want one). She said, "Women do it all the time so why not you." She had a point. She also possessed a nice, clear singing voice and she would go around singing What's Your Name (Don & Juan). So all I did was reverse mine; I went from Forrest Steven to Steven Forrest. The change wasn't really a change at all to me. It just made official what had always seemed natural.

A couple months later I received a confirmation inquiry letter from the Social Security Administration wanting to know if Steven Forrest and Forrest Steven are one and the same person with the same social security number. I filled out the forms, had them notarized at the bank and sent them back. It was done . . .

Chapter 19: Finding A Job

While reading the want-ads in the Sunday Times, I saw an advertisement that caught my eye so I applied for a job with I.T.T. Aetna on Monday. I filled out the application and had an interview scheduled later that day. I was hired on the spot. I started the next day in the West Covina office where I was trained for several weeks before working in finance and real estate for about two years, and was in line for a nice promotion when Charmaine entered my life again, not romantically, though. I would run into to her occasionally since we both lived in West Covina. She was married with a couple kids and working for DPSS (Department of Public Social Services). She told me she was going to apply for a job with the Superior Court in downtown Los Angeles to become a Court Clerk. I asked her what that was, but she really didn't know. She suggested I also apply. I did since the pay was nearly twice what I was making. Charmaine and I took the written test together on a Saturday in December and went to lunch afterwards. Since she already worked for Los Angeles County, she explained how the exam process worked. There were 100 possible points on the written test, but because I was a veteran, I would receive 10 bonus points. That's why she had contacted me. She knew I would get 10 extra points and would do well. I joked with her about that comment and she told me that she never understood how I got such good grades in school and never studied.

A few weeks later when I received notice of my score in the mail, I called her to see how she did. She said that she didn't do as well as she had hoped, but asked my score. When I told her I didn't know how to interpret the numbers, she asked me what they were. I told her my score was 109.75 and it didn't make any sense to me. She screamed and said, "Damn you. You're in." With a 10 point bonus, I had scored 99.75 out of 100 on the written test, plus 10 bonus points to total 109.75, the highest score of the 4000+ people who took the exam. I was #1 on the list. To celebrate, we met for lunch at the Silver Dragon, a Chinese Restaurant in West Covina that we used to frequent when we were going together. She told me I would be contacted soon for an interview, probably downtown somewhere; she was genuinely happy for me and wished me luck with the interview. As we were leaving I smiled at her and said, "I knew you when . . ." She didn't know what I meant. After a brief pause I said, "Thank you." (I Knew You When—Billy Joe Royal)

Chapter 20: A New Profession

In February 1975 I was invited to an oral interview in downtown Los Angeles at the county courthouse. The place was massive. There were only two people present to conduct the interview, an older gentleman named Pete Talmachoff and a young woman from HR. She was there to make sure all my personal information was correct. Mr. Talmachoff was one of the big-wigs in court management, although I didn't know it at the time. My interview consisted of just two questions. First, and before any question was posed to me, I was given a scenario where I had worked for the same judge for a few years and had a fairly good idea of how the judge would rule on a certain case.

Question #1: "What would you say if one of the attorneys in the case being heard in your courtroom asked your opinion of how the judge would rule on the case?" After a moment, my response was short and simple. "I would tell the attorney that he should know better than to ask me that question." That was sort of a 'cop-out' answer so there was a follow-up question that needed a straightforward and succinct answer; it was the question and answer that got me the job.

Questions #2: "Okay. What would you do or say if the attorney persisted?" The interviewer was looking me straight in the eye and my response was curt and blunt. "If he persisted, I'd stand up and tell him to stick it in his ear." How was I to know what to say? Later I found out the type of person hired for the job would have to have a strong personality and act as a buffer between the judge, attorneys, the news media and anyone else trying to get close to him. (Good job, Steven ! ! !)

Shortly thereafter, I gave notice at my job with Aetna. That same night I received a long-distance telephone call from the Aetna corporate offices in St. Louis wanting to know why I was throwing away a promising career. I politely told them I loved my position with Aetna, but I was in it for the money. The job I was taking paid nearly twice as much as I made at Aetna; they offered to match the salary, but it was too late.

On the morning of April 28, 1975, I started the Court Clerk training class in downtown Los Angeles and I relished every minute of it. Although the class was only 8 weeks in length, I found the topics and discussions mesmerizing and I soaked it all in like a sponge. A whole new, captivating world was opening before my eyes. There was just one person in the class who had not previously worked for the Los Angeles County in the past: me. At the end of the class, I was the top candidate and because of that I did not receive an assignment to a judge when I graduated. Instead, I was relegated to a traveling assignment as my instructor informed me during the exit interview that I was the only candidate who showed any 'fire' (sound familiar?), and because of that, I was informed that management wanted to get me greater exposure to the court. For that reason, I was sent traveling around the different courthouses in Los Angeles County acquiring a greater depth of knowledge about the legal system where I would make my new profession lasting 30+ years. (On The Road Again—Willie Nelson)

I had a new job and a new profession, but was still heavily involved in bowling. In fact, I led the San Gabriel Valley classic league in average for two years running. On March 22, 1975, little more than a month before I started with the courts, I bowled the first (and only) 300 game in the San Gabriel Valley Men's Association Tournament. That may not seem significant until you learn that the San Gabriel Valley Men's Bowling Association was founded in 1924, 51 years earlier and never a 300 game. Not until your dad did the deed.

Congratulations

Steve Forrest		Bob Kennicutt
246		202
300		247
195		201
741	1391	650
	66 Hdc.	
	1457	

1st place doubles in the S.G.V. City Tournament. Both using balls drilled at

Mike Fessler's Pro Shop

601 So. San Gabriel, San Gabriel 285-6550

Perfect Game

Chris has the gold and diamond ring the American Bowling Congress (ABC) presented me at the association banquet later in the summer. The American Bowling Congress name and logo no longer exist, replaced by the new name of the United States Bowling Congress.

Although the ring meant a great deal to me, it meant more to me to give it to my son as he never had the opportunity to see his dad bowl. Except for professionals, 300 games in bowling are few and far between. I was fortunate enough to have 15 of them over the years. The interesting thing about my 300 games is that I always made the last shot. That's not a conceited statement, just a fact. Many bowlers have gotten the first 11 strikes in a row only to fail on the final attempt for one reason or another, usually nerves. Well, each time I had the first 11 strikes, I got the 12th one also. Certainly luck also enters the picture and my success in that regard is simple: stay relaxed and confident, but mostly relaxed. I would always say, "Trust is a must or your game is a bust." A little luck of course, but a great deal of trust. I recall a 10-game tournament at Alhambra Valley Bowl in the early 1970s where I was leading the tournament going into the final game. A local pro named Frank Belfour was only 15 pins behind me. Frank bowled 278 his final game, but it wasn't enough.

Reminiscing:
Success in bowling had always come easy and I made many friends because of that success, but it wasn't necessarily a good thing. My ego was swollen and there were times when I needed double doors just to get into a building. A few of the locals from Alhambra Valley Bowl would venture up to San Gabriel Lanes (where I worked after attending UCLA and before my job with the court) to challenge in the local pot games: Dennis Harold, Bill Marks, Rick Turiace, Tom Conlee, and Jim Morris. I smile as I remember some of those contests. This wasn't always so, but it seemed that every time I needed one or two strikes in the last frame, I would get them. A group of us were hanging out and 'shooting the breeze' afterwards when Bill Marks said he was getting tired of me beating them in the late going; Dennis Harold chimed in by saying they didn't come up to San Gabriel Lanes to lose, they came to lose to me. It was quite a complement. Rick Turiace would later become my roommate and close friend. Tom Conlee was an outstanding water skier, but he would always be late for anything, except bowling. He became known as "Never-On-Time Tom." Someone once said it took Tom 20 minutes to fix a salad that was already made.

Another notable incident happened at San Gabriel Lanes on a Sunday afternoon in another pot game. Rick Turiace, then my roommate, was bowling ahead of me and he started his game with 9 strikes in a row, but he was never in front as I matched him strike for strike and in the 10th frame Rick stopped. I didn't. Another 300 game. Sounds like I had lots of 300 games and I guess that's true, but I bowled for nearly 20 years.

A few weeks later at Bowling Square in Pasadena, Rick had the high score in a pot and the only person who could beat him was me and I needed 3 strikes in the last frame to do it, and Rick loudly let everyone know it. In the 10th frame I threw 3 strikes and beat Rick by 2 pins. He yelled at me, "You stiff!" That was his favorite expression to voice his frustration, then he threw his towel up in the air and walked into the bar. Later in the bar, he said, "I don't EVER want to bowl in a game with you again, you never miss." That wasn't quite true. There were plenty of times when I didn't win, but the ones I did win more than made up for them.

Bowling was a big part of my life for nearly 20 years so I'll just add the last items to this journey and then close it here. I voluntarily ended my bowling career in 1979 and the next few pages are from that year. I was a member of the Village Lanes team.

Columbia Bowl, Inc.

PHONE (213) 357-7378

DUARTE, CALIFORNIA 91010
2323 E HUNTINGTON DRIVE

WEEK 18 OF 33 + SWEEPS
SCRATCH

S. G. V. MEN'S CLASSIC

FRIDAY   9:00 PM
01/05/79

NO	TEAM	WON	LOST	PINS	H. G.	H. S.
9	VILLAGE LANES	36.0	18.0	54137	1224	3453
2	PELLEGRINO'S	35.0	19.0	54591	1188	3269
7	ROBBY AUTO POSITIONER	34.0	20.0	54433	1163	3368
3	VALLEY BOWLING SUPPLY	33.0	21.0	53945	1144	3185
12	STATE FARM INS.	29.5	24.5	53593	1187	3282
4	WESTERN COLUMBIA	27.0	27.0	52892	1150	3223
5	COLUMBIA BOWL	25.5	28.5	53997	1189	3267
10	BUD WHIT'S MACH. CO.	25.0	29.0	52108	1125	3102
8	ALHAMBRA VALLEY LANES	22.0	32.0	52147	1104	3212
11	JACK HENNEY CONSTR.	21.0	33.0	51503	1072	3110
1	DOC'S PRO SHOP	19.0	35.0	51797	1135	3184
6	DEXTER'S AUTOMOTIVE	17.0	37.0	52556	1188	3168
		324.0	324.0			

******** SERIES   SEASON HIGH SCORES   GAME ********

VILLAGE LANES	3453	TEAM	COLUMBIA BOWL	1189
HOCKERSMITH, W	834	MEN SCR	HOCKERSMITH, W.	299

TEAM RESULTS

TEAM 10	940- 954-1058-2952 (1.0)	TEAM 7	1150-1019- 921-3090 (1.0)
TEAM 2	1079-1035- 985-3099 (2.0)	TEAM 5	1080-1177- 999-3256 (2.0)
TEAM 11	934- 915- 928-2777 (0.0)	TEAM 12	1132-1031-1119-3282 (2.0)
TEAM 3	995-1018- 932-2945 (3.0)	TEAM 4	912-1056-1018-2986 (1.0)
TEAM 9	1063-1046- 964-3073 (3.0)	TEAM 8	1011-1010- 924-2945 (2.0)
TEAM 1	992- 999- 941-2932 (0.0)	TEAM 6	930- 967- 976-2873 (1.0)

***** HONOR ROLL *****

SCHMIDT, BILL	259-257-216- 732	WELCH, BOB	225-255-208- 688
MOORE, DICK	220-279-210- 709	MYERS, BILLY	192-225-269- 686

*** SCHEDULE ***

LANES   13-14 15-16 17-18 19-20 21-22 23-24

01/12/79 11- 7 9-12 1- 8 5-10 6- 4 3- 2
01/19/79 12- 8 1- 6 10- 7 11- 2 5- 3 9- 4

BLUE CHIP BOWLING, FRIDAY, 12:30!
HAPPY HOUR WEEKDAYS 11-5!

Village Lanes Team #1

81

Steven Forrest

```
WEEK 18 OF 33 + SWEEPS                                          FRIDAY    9:00 PM
SCRATCH                        S.Q.V. MEN'S CLASSIC             01/05/79
```

#	NAME	GA	TP	HG	HS	AVG
7	HOCKERSMITH, W	30	6689	296	834	222
9	FORREST, STEVE	45	9903	276	768	220
3	BURKE, BOB	48	10207	270	702	212
5	SCHMIDT, BILL	21	4451	259	732	211
7	STEINWAY, CHUCK	51	10716	279	720	210
6	ROWLAND, TOM	48	10114	269	763	210
2	BAYER, KENNY	54	11289	276	724	209
9	MORRIS, JIM	48	9929	279	713	206
8	PRESTON, BOB	48	9881	268	674	205
2	WEAVER, DENNIS	54	11021	247	704	204
4	DUNN, JIM	54	11016	258	707	204
6	BURDICK, JERRY	48	9801	290	719	204
2	STANGELO, RICH	47	9600	257	693	204
5	MATHIS, DAN	42	8594	264	688	204
10	MONAGHAN, JACK	54	10988	268	704	203
5	CORTEZ, ALEX	51	10348	257	724	202
9	ZEITS, BOB	42	8524	259	709	202
12	KEEN, JOHN	39	7914	258	688	202
4	MOORE, DICK	54	10884	279	709	201
3	SEARS, DAVE	51	10210	269	702	200
9	GODDARD, ART	30	5986	254	710	199
1	EDIS, DAVE	51	10125	269	683	198
5	PERKINS, MARK	51	10110	267	685	198
8	TROSEN, GARY	54	10672	278	665	197
12	GUY, EARL	51	10052	268	701	197
1	BROSNAN, TIM	51	10042	254	688	196
2	MOSLEY, KEN	51	10038	267	657	196
3	FITZGERALD, JIM	54	10556	277	733	195
6	DEXTER, DON	54	10545	245	664	195
12	WELCH, BOB	42	8221	279	688	195
12	GALLOWAY, LARRY	33	6447	236	640	195
2	BEAUCHAMP, JIM	54	10516	269	701	194
7	BONTA, MIKE	51	9943	249	653	194
11	HUERTA, ANGELO	48	9332	257	670	194
1	LAWRENCE, JIM	48	9330	247	697	194
4	ULRICH, JIM	54	10462	265	744	193
7	PINKOCZI, STEVE	51	9866	258	655	193
1	HARNER, BRUCE	48	9293	246	642	193
10	AVON, DICK	51	9802	236	622	19
1	CASEY, JIM	48	9229	280	696	19
8	PUGLISI, DON	48	8092	247	665	19
11	RARDON, LARRY	54	10316	258	651	191
10	DUMOND, CHUCK	53	10140	242	639	191
8	ALLEN, LEW	48	9170	236	649	191
10	MYERS, BILLY	37	7097	269	686	191
8	BLAESING, ELMER	54	10286	249	657	190
11	JAROSZ, STEVE	51	9732	255	696	190
11	COVELL, BOB	48	9135	248	619	190
12	STRUCK, RICHARD	54	10257	246	679	189
4	KNAPP, TOM	44	8402	279	744	190
4	WILLIAMSON, ED	51	9638	256	670	188
5	FIELDS, STEVE	45	8472	261	645	188
11	PRECHTL, DAVE	54	10056	243	635	186
8	ATWOOD, GARY	54	10058	245	637	185
6	FAIRFIELD, ROY	51	9475	254	636	185
10	WHIT, BUD	42	7776	222	603	185
1	CURISH, STEVE	30	5528	232	612	184
6	FERGUSON, BILL	51	9261	257	629	181
9	CREAMER, BILL	26	4632	235	612	178

*** SUBSTITUTES ***

NAME	GA	TP	HG	HS	AVG
BADERDEEN, GREG	6	1252	256	675	208
BELLO, JOHN	3	570	193	539	179
BORDENAVE, JEROME	33	6590	277	635	190
BULLEN, STEVE	6	1138	213	582	189
CONNOR, TOM	12	2194	228	605	182
FENTON, BOB	6	1157	237	596	192
HARDING, ERNIE	12	2565	249	693	213
KASPER, ROBIN	20	3700	225	599	185
LEE, DAVE	3	498	189	498	166
LOVE, GARY	1	201	201	201	201
MELLICK, BILL	3	637	217	637	212
NELSON, WARREN	12	2534	249	688	211
PRATT, JOHN	3	539	202	539	179
SAMSON, SAM	1	189	189	189	189
SISLOFSKY, RUSSELL	3	584	208	584	194
TROSEN, FLOYD	3	570	196	570	190
TURNER, MIKE	30	5969	278	716	198
WILCOX, FRANK	9	1712	210	576	190
FESSLER, MIKE	38	7465	248	669	196
LINDSEY, BUD	9	1658	216	590	184
JONES, BUD	3	584	235	584	194
STAGGERS, TIM	3	541	192	541	180
DOBIN, RON	0	582	195	582	194
SHIRLEY, BILL	1	119	119	119	119
BELLINDER, FRANK	18	3660	259	683	203
BENSON, ROB	3	624	232	624	206
BRYCE, BRUCE	6	1081	191	554	180
BYRNE, MIKE	12	2396	248	619	199
COOPER, JIM	12	2387	198	681	198
HANSEN, DENNIS	3	565	199	565	188
JONES, CURT	12	2491	256	643	207
KENNICUTT, BOB	4	817	239	607	204
LENTINE, QIP	9	1989	300	759	221
MALETTA, JOHN	21	4533	278	696	215
MILLER, BING	6	1055	202	550	175
NIETO, LARRY	3	535	199	535	178
RUTHERFORD, DAN	1	137	137	137	137
SCOTT, DICK	3	338	192	538	179
TAYLOR, LARRY	9	1749	223	641	194
TURIACE, RICK	9	1646	207	571	182
VANHEES, KELLY	9	1800	247	648	200
WINGERT, RALPH	24	5011	268	713	208
LUXTON, ROYCE	3	548	191	548	182
YOUNGBLOOD, COY	3	617	215	617	205
SURKO, DEAN	3	500	166	500	166
KNIGHT, DOUG	3	622	226	622	207
FEZZLER, MIKE	6	1192	246	630	198

Bowler's Averages

Chapter 21: Miss Penny

During my travels around the different courthouses on various assignments, I had the pleasure of meeting a very attractive and friendly lady working at the Filing Window at the Pasadena Courthouse. Her name was Penny Jones and she had a beautifully warm smile and a soft personality. My stay in Pasadena was a week long and I talked with Penny often and asked her out at the end of the week. Soon Penny was accompanying me on Friday nights when I bowled in the San Gabriel Valley Classic League at Bahama Lanes in Pasadena. When my teammate, Ed Williamson, saw Penny for the first time, he walked up to me and whispered in my ear, "Outstanding!" I knew what he meant. Penny was very attractive with auburn hair and bright, dazzling green eyes, and she possessed a smile that was instantly disarming. She and I went everywhere together and my moments with her were joyful, loving and always fun. She was quite a lady, but again, something seemed to be missing. (Green-Eyed Lady—Sugarloaf)

Penny had a 7-year old daughter, Paula Christine Jones. She was playful, bubbly and full of life. As a matter of fact, the first time I met Paula, she ran up to me (I was sitting on Penny's front porch) and said, "Hi, daddy." Those were the first words Paula spoke to me, but I was too naive to recognize the danger signs. Penny was living with Paula in a small, rented house in Pasadena and I lived with my buddy, Rick Turiace, in an apartment in Alhambra, just eight miles away. At one time, Rick was one of the "bat boys" for the Los Angeles Dodgers which translated to Dodger games "on the house."

Penny wasn't interested in sports, but we enjoyed movies, dinners, and just hanging out. She accompanied me when I bowled, but paid little attention to the game although she was gregarious and fit in well with the other ladies. In February 1976, Penny told me she was pregnant and we needed to talk. Stunned and silent, I grew restless with knots in my stomach.

> "Well I tried to make it Sunday, but I got so damn depressed,
> That I set my sights on Monday and I got myself undressed,
> I ain't ready for the altar but I do agree there's times,
> When a woman sure can be a friend of mine."
>
> . . . America

I wouldn't walk away this time. Making the best of a bad situation and even worse judgment, Penny and I were married in Las Vegas. Eight months later, Christopher Steven Forrest was born on October 27, 1976, in Pasadena; he was a bicentennial baby and has a red, white & blue birth certificate to prove it. His birth was made by special appointment. With Paula's birth, Penny had a C-Section. So too with Chris. There were now 4 of us and we needed more space. Within a few months, we would buy our first and only home. Our relationship was like a whirlwind and there were many things about Penny I was yet to discover although she was just 27 years old: multiple previous marriages and multiple abortions. Her past was her past and I didn't pass judgment on it, yet I often wondered about the abortions.

A few months later, I was working at the Norwalk Courthouse in a criminal trial court, assigned to Judge Ralph A. Biggerstaff. Prior to this new assignment, Judge Biggerstaff interviewed several candidates for the open position; he said he was looking for a Court Clerk who would NOT be here today and gone tomorrow. I told him if were selected, I would remain his Court Clerk until he retired. The job was mine and that commitment lasted nearly 12 years. I passed up promotions a number of times and when managers asked me why, I told them I made a commitment that I intended to keep. At the beginning of 1977, Judge Biggerstaff was elevated to the position of Supervising Judge and assigned to Department A. He was now the Master Calendar Judge which meant he had control of the entire courthouse, although Supervising Judges do not normally interfere with other judge's courtrooms. The good thing about the Master

Calendar department was the exposure to all types of litigation AND no more trials. There was no downside and I greatly enjoyed everything I was learning and was eager for any challenge. My time as a Superior Court Clerk was the most enjoyable job I ever had, challenging at times, yet very rewarding. I could not have stumbled into a better profession (thank you, Charmaine).

One afternoon, Judge Biggerstaff was hearing a divorce case and the parties involved had to sell their home in West Covina as part of the settlement they were negotiating. The attorneys both said they would seek a buyer ASAP and I mentioned to them I may be interested. After work that day, I drove out to West Covina to 1021 Eclipse Way. It was a 4-bedroom, 2-bath house with a huge 19'x 36' pool in the back. The front of the house had white brick and black wrought-iron fencing. I made an offer of $52,000 which was accepted. Within a month we moved to West Covina.

I was still bowling in tournaments and the very best, most competitive bowling leagues. Our team in the classic league at Bahama Lanes finished 2nd to the Pelligrino's team in 1976. Our team sponsor, as well as my individual sponsor, was Western Columbia, distributor of Columbia Bowling balls and other sports equipment. Western Columbia is located on San Gabriel Boulevard in San Gabriel, just down the street from San Gabriel Lanes.

The San Gabriel Valley Classic League moved from Bahama Lanes in Pasadena to Columbia Bowl in Duarte for the 1976-77 season, and with the move came a new sponsor, Village Lanes which was owned and operated by Art Goddard, one of my teammates. Our team won the Classic league in '77, '78 & '79. We had a powerful roster that included Bob Zeits (the Zipper), Bob Kennicutt (my doubles partner), Mike Fessler (the Pooh) and Art Goddard (AG). Bob Kennicutt was the best bowler I ever knew. He was a gentle man, short in stature at about 5'8", but what a competitor. He won many local tournaments, but never ventured out on the PBA tour. He was a family man. When I bowled 300 in the SGVA Tournament in 1975, Kennicutt (my doubles partner) bowled 247 the same game. Our doubles score of 547 was the highest doubles game in California and the 2nd highest doubles game in the country that year. Mike Fessler had finished 2nd in the ABC Masters a few years earlier, but had health problems. Art Goddard was a 200 average bowler who owned and operated several bowling establishments. Our team set many team records at Columbia Bowl, including a high game of 1224 and 3453 3-game set. Those records may not still be standing, but when we set them, the old records were not just beaten, they were smashed. I led the league in average my last two years, setting a personal high of 215 in 1979, my last year. Bowling then was a bit more difficult than it is today. Back then the lanes were not synthetic and the bowling balls were rubber. Acrylic bowling balls and synthetic lanes were just being developed. Enough reminiscing about bowling . . .

And now on to the most important segment on this journey and Leo Buscaglia, the man who changed my life . . .

Chapter 22: Buscaglia—the man who changed my life

In the spring of 1979 and purely by accident I had the pleasure of attending a lecture conducted by a professor of philosophy from USC (of all places) named Leo Buscaglia. I recorded that lecture and even though the recording isn't always clear, I have listened to it more times than I care to recall. Dr. Buscaglia's words brought tears to my eyes that day and touched tender feelings deep inside me. He was the most charismatic person I've yet to meet. After the lecture, I had an opportunity to speak with him for a few moments before he was whisked off to meet others. His hand shake was warm and genuine and his manner was openly inviting. Unexpectedly, while I was trying to formulate a relevant question, he interrupted me and said, "Excuse me for interrupting, but I can see where you're going with this. Happiness, young man, is a choice, always a choice. You can choose to be happy or choose to be sad. It's YOUR choice, no one else's." And then he was gone. That response left me in intense and provocative thought for the longest time, and would eventually lead to a change in my behavior from one who always looked toward himself to the person who would later project out to others. That transformation was slow and gradual, and over the years I became more tolerant (although Chris and Alicia may not think so).

> "I could teach everyone in this room everything I know, and I would still know what I know. I would have lost nothing."
> . . . Leo Buscaglia

Leo Buscaglia, PhD, the author of books such as Living, Loving and Learning and Born for Love, renowned lecturer, and University of Southern California professor, touched untold numbers with his insights into how we seek happiness and create loving relationships. Instantly impressive is how I would describe Buscaglia, and if you have listened to my recording of that lecture you would know that is not his real name. Understandably, it would take some time before I would grasp the concepts he discussed that day, but my direction in life was changing and for the first time it was changing for the better as I finally started to mature, and it only took 34 years. I set out my new path in life to mentor, although I have not always been successful at it. My personality changed as I realized the world did not revolve around me and I was not the center of attention after all. Listening to Buscaglia provided a more profound insight on what is actually important in life and what is not. After reading LOVE (What Life Is Really About), my emotions softened as did my outward temperament; I would read several more of his books and each touched my soul.

> "To be fully functioning, we must be as welcoming of the new as we are comfortable with the old, as fearless of the unexpected as we are falsely secure in the planned."
> . . . Leo Buscaglia

According to Dr. Buscaglia, love is patient and kind; love is not jealous, or conceited, or proud; love is not ill-mannered, or selfish, or irritable; love does not keep a record of wrongs; love is not happy with evil, but is happy with the truth. Love never gives up; its faith, hope and patience will never fail. Love is eternal . . . There are faith, hope and love, these three, but the greatest of these is love.

The most important lesson Dr. Buscaglia taught was how to "let go" when unhappiness and stressful situations tighten their unmerciful grip on your life. The topical theme for his talk that day was People Helping People and his manner and explosively touching personal tone captured the attention of most everyone in attendance. It certainly did mine. He went on to explain that there was so much to do to make this a better world that he felt incapacitated, until he understood that it was not what "we" could do, but what "I" could do to make the world a better place. He said something that day about personal relationships that is an axiom in life:

"You have the capacity to love, a limitless capacity to love, but unless you learn how, you'll never realize it . . .

You can only give to others what you have. If you have nothing, you give nothing. You can only teach what you know. If all you know is fear and ugliness and pain and prejudice, you will teach it everywhere you go. If you know beauty and joy and spirituality, you will teach beauty and joy and spirituality to everyone in your life space. But you have to have it first!

The wonderful thing about these concepts that are not tangible: you can't touch 'em, you can't bank 'em, you can't list them. They're there. You can't sell 'em and they can't be bought. They can only be given freely. But in the process of giving freely, you never lose it."

. . . Leo Buscaglia

It took quite a while to digest his words and I have not always practiced what he offered that day, but his impact on my life has been remarkably substantial. There have been difficult moments in my life when I reached for that tape to ease my way through troubled times. Learning is oftentimes painful and I found myself at odds with my wasteful past and what I wanted in the future. He closed his lecture with a statement written by an 85 year old man who was a terminal patient that is a strongly moving preview on what he would do if he had the chance to live his life over again. There is a great lesson to be learned from it, so I'll quote it at the conclusion of my story.

"If you don't like the stage you're on, surround yourself with new actors and start over again." Thanks to Dr. Buscaglia, my mind broke free from the bindings of my past and I began a genesis to a more caring person, not as one possessed by delusional entitlement. Consequently, I did a number of things I thought I would never do. First, I quit bowling. Second, I quit gambling. The Classic League ended in May 1979. I remember well my final 3-game set on the lanes: 692 (225-235-232). I had finished the SGV Mens Classic League as the #1 bowler and I was at the top of my game. And I just walked away. I quit bowling, cold turkey, because it just wasn't good for me. For my parting gesture, I took my gear (bowling ball, bag and shoes) to the Vincent Thomas Bridge in San Pedro and dropped them into the ocean. That was more than 30 years ago and to this day, I have not walked into a bowling center anywhere. That chapter of my life was over and I decided to make the best of a bad situation and search out new and more positive adventures. I was letting go of those things that were not good for me, and I thank Buscaglia for teaching me the way. One of them was Penny . . . (I Will Survive—Gloria Gaynor)

Thanks to Felicé Leonardo Buscaglia, a butterfly launched itself from the grips of its cocoon, free to fly and make the best of a short, sweet and wonderful life. If there was just one lesson I could 'download' to my children, it would be my endearing relationship to this marvelous man and his piercing manner of teaching others about love.

This chapter is very dear to me and I am going to tell you both another truth in life. There will be times in your life when you will inadvertently absolutely crush someone emotionally. Read that again. Whether you intend to do so or not will not matter. You will do it, and it will be done to you. Life is not a fair game, but it can be filled with joy and peace and happiness. Most of all, it can be filled with love. I surely hope so for you both.

The thousand dreams I dreamed, the splendid things I planned
I always built to last on weak and shifting sand,
I lived by night and shunned the naked light of the day
And only now I see how the years ran away . . .

. . . Roy Clark

Chapter 23: Confessions

Have you ever felt that you have been trapped by guilt? That unnerving feeling has haunted me since my Army days. Guilt is the core element that disenables me from fully sharing or participating in family matters and is responsible, in so many ways, for much of my emotional impotence. In his younger years, your dad was the master of "wrong" for just about anything and everything. Why do you suppose I'm telling you this? Because I would give just about anything to spare you from this self-destructive emotion, and yet I know I cannot. Most of the time, I'm quite the positive guy so don't get the wrong impression from what I am saying. It's just that some of the mistakes I have blundered through simply bring on an eerily uncomfortable feeling and tears well-up in my eyes when I reflect on them. Even though I consider myself an emotionally stable man, I am intentionally open to vulnerability and human feelings. It's the reflection that causes the guilt in me; sort of a catch 22 that has transcended time. "Steven, you're an idiot." That statement is just so true and it's my favorite way to describe myself at times. On the other hand . . .

Felicé Leonardo Buscaglia taught me to "let go" of those things where the pieces of the puzzle don't fit. "Don't torture yourself when you have no control. Stop lashing out at others; you're only hurting yourself. Be nicer. I don't know if anyone has ever told you this, but you are the best you and that's all you've got," he would say. Even as my working career was succeeding, my relationship with Penny was not. We were quickly growing apart for a number of reasons, but I'll step up here and tell you flatly the failure of our relationship was purely mine. Of course it always takes two to make it or break it, and I realized that fact all too clearly. In this instance, however, Penny was blameless. Her personality and mine didn't overlap. Besides, there was something missing (she wasn't Susan). So I'll just let it go at that.

We went our separate ways in late 1979. With my marriage on the rocks, I was an empty shell, and yet I somehow managed not to let it show outwardly because of great camouflage. Openly, I admit that the experience was a very profound and emotionally painful one, and I detested myself because of the hurt I had caused others, especially the children. They were blameless and scared, and, yes, Steven was still an idiot. Perhaps in the past I would have raised the barriers of emotional self-protection, but I didn't. Not anymore. There was just too much pain in my past and it would be my choice on how to deal with it. Happy or sad, it would be my choice.

Here I was an educated man (not a wise one), a stellar athlete, and a very affable individual, but I was a flat out failure at the important areas of life. There was a vast empty space in my life I just could not fill, no matter the effort. I would do or had done many of the right things for the wrong reasons and because I was an emotional disaster searching for a place to happen, sometimes I did nothing which was just as bad. I wanted help and I needed a hero, so I clung to Buscaglia's books and read and reread them. As I let go of my relationship with Penny, I understood we were not good for each other and it was a marriage that had taken place because of poor judgment and even poorer foresight. There was nothing wrong with her; the wrong was "us." I discovered another of my several imperfections as I had again failed at a personal relationship by trampling on feelings, those delicate jewels comprising a piece of one's personality, but vowed to do my best to repair the harm I had brought. Placing the blame squarely where it belonged (with myself) I was strong enough to realize the pain and discomfort I had caused others and I began to act on my new found beliefs. It would be nearly 10 years before I would take another unsuccessful stab at a lasting relationship. When I did, I did everything right in my opinion, to no avail. And that should be a beacon that nothing is ever guaranteed. I would remain open and vulnerable and give free access to my feelings, and I would try again, and again, and again, never to give up. As Buscaglia would say, "Without love in your heart, you have nothing, no dreams, no faith, no hope." Just like my mom, I am and always will be a dreamer.

Initially, Penny left to live with her cousin, Carol, in Pasadena. Carol and I were like oil and water and didn't care for each other and we both let the other know it. She had big teeth and huge legs so I gave her the friendly name of "thunder thighs." I had other unpleasant names for her that will remain unannounced. Yeah, I was maturing alright, just not as well as I had hoped. Still had a ways to go, a long ways to go. Carol and Penny were heavily into the women's lib thing going on at the time and any discussions with them were highly charged. When Penny moved out, she left her daughter, Paula, and Chris with me. With Penny gone, I had the absolute pleasure of caring for two scrappy youngsters. Paula was 10 and Christopher was not yet 3, but we made the best of it and over the next few months we had some amazingly wonderful outings together.

One afternoon we were off to the movies for the first showing of the Lucas/Spielberg Star Wars follow-up film "The Empire Strikes Back." The film was playing at the Cinerama Dome Theater in Hollywood. My little people were uncontrollably excited, as was I. Adults came to see the movie, but most of the movie-goers were teenagers and kids. In her excitement at being there, Paula was running and jumping around much like the Energizer Bunny, like a little wind-up toy that explodes everywhere and takes the path of least resistance. She couldn't contain herself. Because he was so small, Chris sat on my shoulders as we waited for our showing and he kept giggling and laughing; he and I laughed a lot. We were a playful threesome. Yeah, those were happy moments and I quietly smile when I reflect on them.

On most weekends, Penny would take one of the kids, but the schedule she kept was erratic at best. One weekend, she took them both, which was unusual, and called me Sunday evening as I was expecting them home. She paused and finally said she wasn't bringing them back to me, instead they would stay with her and Carol in Pasadena. All I could manage to say was, "Take good care of them." (I'm Sorry—Brenda Lee)

Absent was the fierce, competitive and defiant spirit I had known since my youth. Oh, it was still there (and always will be), residing under the surface. In its place, however, a quiet calmness was emerging as I searched to find Penny's point of view. What would I have done if I were her? That's not an easy question for someone with a large ego to answer and so I gave it a considerable amount of thought, and the answer touched a nerve that caused a great deal of discontent and a very uneasy feeling. I didn't like what I was seeing . . .

> Yesterday the moon was blue
> And every crazy day brought something new to do.
> I used my magic age as if it were a wand
> And never saw the waste and emptiness beyond . . .

Chapter 24: Vanessa

"To cheat oneself out of love is the most terrible deception; it is an eternal loss for which there is no reparation, either in time or eternity."

. . . Kierkegaard

"Time wounds all heals," is timeless and my life was moving along at a leisurely pace in the early part of 1980 when I received a telephone call with news that hit like a brick. My little step-sister, Vanessa, had been in a car accident on the 210 Freeway in Glendora. She did not survive. It had happened again, and unfortunately, not for the last time. Of all Dolores' children, the only one I was close to was Vanessa. She and I had a special bond that was the envy of the family and I protected her fiercely the little time we had together. Vanessa was a tiny, little thing, barely 5 feet tall and about 90 pounds, but she was a beauty to behold with a personality that matched. Jokingly, I often called her "the bridesmaid" and she would slap me on the shoulder for saying it. Other times I would tease her and tell her she didn't even weigh a dollar. Another whack! Vanessa had entered many beauty contests as a teenager and had finished runner-up nearly each time. On her untimely death (she was only 21), I must have shown my extremely unhappy emotional state at work, because one of the ladies noticed and asked me about it. Her name was Reneé Kay. She and I were close friends and she used to date my roommate Dave. I poured it all out to her and the genuine understanding she freely gave lifted my spirits, although it took some time. At Vanessa's funeral, I brought 21 yellow roses with a beautiful card that summed up my true personal feelings for my young, departed step-sister. It read, "Thank you for touching my life. You were my sunshine when there was none." Those words cling to my memories of her and still bring a loving tear . . .

Vanessa (bottom left)

With an empty heart and an empty house with a big pool, I felt the only way to go was up. Once again I was down in the dumps, but life went on as it always does, waiting for no one. Life is for the living and I heard Buscaglia's voice: "Let it go." I did, but not before Vanessa was comfortable. The cemetery in Covina where she was buried was neat, clean and very well-maintained with plenty of large oak trees and beautiful lush gardens, except the grass was brown. For weeks I carried 5-gallon bottles of water and ammonium sulfate to her grave site and commenced my gardening project. Sounds silly, doesn't it? No one knows I did this, and no one knows I sat quietly with her for hours and talked endlessly without saying a word. After nearly a month of almost daily watering and care, there was a very bright green patch of grass in the cemetery (the only one) and I felt better for it. I'm sure she did, too . . .

Chapter 25: When You Least Expect It . . .

Ya know, for me this has been an interestingly positive adventure so far as I picture myself doing the laundry of my life, shaking out the memories and letting them dry in the crisp mountain air. Feels kinda good so I'm going to take a moment here and make another offering of life's trappings, one that you won't realize until it happens to you, and it will.

At some point in your life, probably when you least expect it, you are going to experience emotional pain in such a debilitating manner that you will feel completely helpless and most likely worthless, and deep into your cave you will flee with your emotional barriers to protect you. Perhaps others around you will see it, perhaps not, but you will feel emptiness in your soul. I know; I've been there. Man, have I been there. It's part of life's journey and at some point in yours you may believe, truly believe, that you are the perfect person or perfect "banana" for someone you care about deeply. However perfect you may be, some people are allergic to bananas. Believe me when I tell you that it won't be your fault. It's just the way things seem to happen, and again there are no guarantees when dealing with your emotions. After the passage of time and some painful emotional healing, you will come creeping out of your shell, your cave so to speak. But before you start climbing out from the abyss, make sure it's empty, completely empty and leave nothing there to regret. Remember: "Time wounds all heals."

With Vanessa gone, once again my life seemed in the bottom of the barrel, but I did the best I could and emptied everything out, everything except the longing for the one I left behind so many years before. That state of emptiness still lingers with me, even though I have managed my life better than most. And that's the point I trying to get across. I had managed my life; I hadn't really lived it to that point, at least not as I had hoped. No one knows as this secret has traveled through time with me and it is one of the silent burdens I carry still, but I would never let the thought of Susan go, even though the thought of seeing her again was a distant, evasive dream. The search for her would not ever cease. I guess you could say it's not a secret anymore.

> Ya know I've heard about people like me,
> But I never made the connection.
> They walk one road to set them free,
> And find they've gone the wrong direction.
>
> ... Don McLean

In the summer of 1980, after Vanessa departed, I acquired two goofy roommates: Dave Cummins and Jerome Bordenave. Over the next year or so the three of us would enjoy life as it came and live in the moment; it was the perfect way to heal and start in a new direction. Dave was a classmate of mine at Baldwin Park High School in 1963 and, of course, we were the same age. As a profession, Dave worked as a mechanic on AMF pin-setters at Keystone Lanes (owned by Art Goddard) in Norwalk. Dave moved in first and he and I would have endless conversations on the downside of life and what we were going to do to change it for the better. I can't recall how many times I have listened to people telling how many problems they had. That is just plain wrong, near-sighted and totally self-destructive. Buscaglia was my guy, my silent mentor and partner, although he never knew that, and because of him I had no problems, only challenges, and I have lived my live that way since I met him. With Dave, I joked about life as a challenge and my always upbeat and positive attitude was rubbing off on my buddy.

Dave was very good at building and fixing things so at a swap meet one Sunday, I bought a Pepsi-Cola vending machine that didn't work for $50. Dave and I got the thing in his VW bus and headed home to West Covina. He fixed the refrigeration unit and we had an instant soda machine that was packed with beer than soda. We had weekend pool-side barbeques and it seemed the place was always packed. Anyone and everyone in the neighborhood were welcome. By the way, they could drink all they wanted as we had our vending machine, 50¢ a drink, quarters only. Jerome attended one of our parties and stayed late one afternoon after everyone else had left. Dave and Jerome hit it off right away. Later that evening Dave took me aside and told me Jerome was having a difficult time and then casually asked if "we" could use another roommate. I chuckled and used a saying from my distant past when I very slowly smiled and said, "Whyyyyyyyy, certainly." With the three of us together, I told Jerome he was invited to join us, but told him his name was just too formal. From now on I would call him "Jay." That was fine with everyone.

Jay worked at Columbia Bowl on Brunswick pin-setters. He was 22 and on his own. Jay, Dave and I became 'Tres Amigos' and hung together most weekends. Dave was recently divorced and bought a Corvette. We were always talking cars and the ones we used to have and what we would get later when the money rolled in. Jay had a red Firebird and he was restoring it and rebuilding the engine. I had an Olds Cutlass, black on black with a smoke grey T-Top.

At that time, country music was making a big impact and everyone became an instant expert on country music, or so they thought. I had been raised on it, and when someone would make a silly or ill-advised comment that was obviously incorrect, I didn't even think of a putdown. I would have in the past. Not anymore. All I would say is, "Amazing," or "Is that so?" Giving and acceptance were becoming an important part of "me," and I would become a lifetime member of the sentimental mush balls. I found life was more enjoyable when the focus was not on me. Imagine that!

Tres Amigos became party animals and we loved to dance (not with each other, though), so we frequented as many establishments as we could find on the weekends with the Cattleman's Wharf in Hacienda Heights our favorite. I hadn't quit drinking all together and set a limit on how much I would drink, 1 beer. I really liked beer, always did. You two may not realize this fact, but I never really drank hard liquor and I never smoked, just beer and sometimes a glass of wine at meals. Ice-cold beer was a staple and a real life-saver on those super-hot water-ski vacations to the desert.

Dave had a girlfriend named Lillian who lived in the foothills of Rowland Heights. I couldn't settle on a girlfriend, so I had lots of them. Jay's girlfriend, Diane, lived in Hacienda Heights and her parents didn't care for him. He was a mulatto; Diane was white. After much debate between Diane and Jay, Diane moved out of her parent's house and in with us. Our house was crowded, but we all liked disco! (Billie Jean—Michael Jackson)

The first gasoline crisis came in 1982 and caused a great deal of confusion and aggravation with almost everyone. Not panicking, I decided something different was needed to address my own concerns over rising gas prices. Now don't laugh, but gasoline jumped from about 39¢ a gallon to 64¢ a gallon in one week and people were stunned and angry. Things got so bad that gasoline was rationed by license plate number. Odd numbers one day, even the next. It was crazy. The Norwalk Courthouse was about 20 miles away and I wasn't about to pay those inflated gas prices, so I purchased a new Schwinn 10-speed and rode it to work, going over the Whittier hills on Colima Road. As it turned out, that didn't work out so well as the brakes on my new bike would not stop me as I came screaming down on the steep part of Colima (ever seen smokin' sneakers?). That evening the new bike went back to Sears, and Steven went hunting for a bike shop. I found one in Hacienda Heights and bought a new La Mans Centurion. That was more like it. I rode my Centurion to work 3 times a week on average and worked my way into even better physical condition. The riding came easy as I skied, both water and snow, played basketball twice a week on Tuesday and Thursday nights, and ran about 10 miles a week. Some of the folks at work thought I was nuts for riding so far to work on a bicycle (20 miles). One winter morning I left for work wearing cut-offs and sneakers (no shirt) and the outside temperature was a brisk 34 degrees. The cold bit deep, but after a few miles steam started rising from my body and people gave me the strangest looks as I pedaled my way on by them. (Maniac—Michael Sembello)

Steve & Tom

To enjoy life to its fullest, I went on winter vacations, following the snow as best I could. On one trip with never-on-time Tom to Lake Tahoe, I switched places with Tom. In the past he was the dare devil, especially when water-skiing. At Lake Mead in Nevada one summer, we dove off of steep cliffs into the water. Most of us were comfortable diving from 30 feet or so, but not Tom. He dove off, head first, from a cliff at least 100 feet above the water. Bad idea. His head hurt for a couple days and although he never complained, he kept calling us sissies. Later though, five of us went off from that same cliff, only feet first. We wore sneakers and it was an incredible experience. It must have looked like we were crazy, five guys holding hands in mid-air screaming on their way down to the water.

Now, however, in the snow, Tom was the wimp. He would follow me to places I probably should not have taken him. Dropping off one cornice about 50 feet, I turned my skis in mid-air and landed softly in the deep snow on the side of the mountain, made a couple of very quick turns and stopped. For Tom, it was a much different outcome. The next day I took Tom down trails only an idiot would try (that fits, doesn't it?). The terrain was steep and icy, but my edges were sharp and I was fearless. Wrong word. I was nuts! But I loved the speed, always did. Poor Tom was all over the place. I became the "go for it" guy on the slopes. Tom told me I was crazy and suffered from brain flush. Maybe so; I wore a bright yellow turtle-neck shirt that read, "No Guts—No Glory."

Later on that trip, we drove to the Kirkwood Ski Resort where I "sort of" had an accident. I was whipping down one of the downhill runs (I thought) and came flying across a road about 20 feet in the air. I went straight into a mogul field (I hated the bumps) and buried my skis up to the bindings and flew out head-first into the snow. As I went face-first into one of the moguls, and my sunglasses split in half as I went flying out of control. I tumbled, flew, spun, and crashed my way down the mountain for a couple hundred yards. In my path I left my gloves, poles, skis, hat and anything else attached to me in a long trail. When I finally came to rest there was no part of me that didn't hurt, but fortunately nothing was broken. A very attractive blonde came up to me and said, "That was GREAT! Can you do it again?" Then she skied away.

Our next trip was to Utah (Snowbird, Alta, and Deer Valley) with even better skiing and many more thrills. We would jump out of snow chutes down into deep powder. Powder was nice, but I didn't care for it as much as I did the downhill runs. Weighting, unweighting and turning in powder was not nearly as much fun as speed. The faster I went, the more I liked it. To get to the chutes, though, we had to take the chair for the "Elevator Shaft" run and then climb up the mountain at Alta. Elevator Shaft was a deep, steep run where we would warm up in the mornings to get our ski legs ready. The name of that run fit perfectly. Tom and I stayed at a hill-side ski resort at Alta. Snowbird, another ski resort, was just down the road. The nice thing about that trip is there were no beginner's runs at Alta or Snowbird. Just Intermediate runs, Advanced runs, and Crazy. We spent a week on the snow from daylight to dusk and had the time of our lives. It was the best ski trip I ever experienced. One evening at the Snowbird resort, we found live entertainment and the band was playing my favorite ski song of all time: Queen of Hearts (Juice Newton). Tom and I hooked up with a couple of cute lady skiers and enjoyed dancing the evening away. I requested the band to play Queen of Hearts several times. I really liked that song. When barreling down a steep run, Queen of Hearts playing on my Walkman kept me balanced and moving . . .

Chapter 26: Unexpected Assistance

Even though I loved living in West Covina, I had spent most of my life in the San Gabriel Valley, I sold my house in the summer of 1985 and moved near the ocean. I wanted a change of environment and found a 3-bedroom, 3-bath townhouse in the rolling hills of Rancho Palos Verdes. For a townhouse it was spacious, over 2000 square feet, and the solitude of the area was refreshing and felt warmly inviting. How I managed to get it is an interesting tale.

Mr. Tom Deihl was an acquaintance of mine at the Norwalk Courthouse. He was an older gentleman, pushing the back side of 70, would was occasionally appointed as a 'master' on Probate matters. There were a number of occasions where I assisted Tom and helped him get the tough Probate orders approved. As part of my responsibilities, I assisted everyone I could and did so happily, always with a warm smile. The "old Steven" was not such a guy, but the "new Steven" was more like it, and I really liked the way I was developing as a person. Mr. Deihl also had a management company and performed work as an 'administrator' or 'estate guardian' in other Probate matters. One morning after the Probate calendar had completed, I mentioned to Tom that I was interested in buying property in Palos Verdes. "Pretty pricy area, Steve," he said. Tom asked if he could ride out and see it with me. Good idea, I thought, since he was an expert on property management.

That evening we rode out to Palos Verdes, stopping for dinner first at Hof's Hut. While eating, Tom told me he wasn't usually impressed with condos or townhouses, but wanted to make sure that things were on the up and up for my benefit. Nice gesture.

After viewing the property, Tom indicated it was a sound investment because of the location and because of the care and maintenance provided, even if it was a townhouse. He suggested we go to Home Savings in Torrance and discuss financing with them. We agreed and Tom called me the next day and asked if I was free to go to Home Savings that evening. Sure thing, I was anxious to find out if I could qualify for the loan as I only made $2800 a month then. The appointment at Home Savings was set for 7:00 p.m. and I didn't think anything of it when Tom called, but then I remembered that banks are not open that late. When we arrived just before 7:00 p.m., Tom drove around the back where we were met by the branch manager. There were just three people there: the branch manager, the loan officer, and someone to type up the forms. Tom said he needed to discuss something with the branch manager and left the room, leaving me with the other two. The loan officer asked how I knew Tom. So I told him. Then he asked me if I knew Tom's brother, Richard Deihl. I didn't. "Richard Deihl, Tom's brother, is Chairman of the Board for Home Savings," he told me. Whoa ! ! !

When the branch manager returned, he said he had three questions for me.

Q: Do you like the property.
A: Yes, of course.

Q: Can you afford $1100 payments?
A: Yes. I have no outstanding debt.

Q: Last question, do you want it?
A: Yes.

"Loan's approved," he said. No application, no credit inquiries, no nothing. Tom had vouched for me and that's all it took. The forms were typed as we waited and escrow closed in just a few days. Can you believe my luck? Later I found out I would not have qualified for the loan unless I could put 25% down, and I didn't have $40,000. No matter.

I spent many quiet evenings just sitting under the pines reading, studying, and listening to country music. My townhouse was located in the far corner of a massive complex with huge 100 feet tall pine trees across the brick drive from my front door. There was a family of skunks living under the townhouse and I would see them occasionally walking in the woods single file. Cute little guys . . .

Chapter 27: Problems, Problems, Problems

This segment is painfully full of sour notes. Over the years Penny and I maintained a friendly relationship even though we had periodic flare-ups over her parenting mishaps. One evening she called me in a panic telling me Paula had run away from home and was staying at a girlfriend's house. Penny was crying and said she didn't know what to do. I asked for the number where I could contact Paula and called her immediately. When she came to the phone, I told Paula she had exactly 30 minutes to get home or she was going to jail; I wasn't bluffing and she knew it. About an hour later Penny called telling me Paula was home and crying. It was becoming clear that although Penny was a sweet person, her parenting skills were severely deficient; she had no control over Paula, and I wasn't so sure about my son. Shortly thereafter I had Paula living with me and I took particular care to make sure she had everything she needed, but there was a surprise coming that I just didn't see. Each morning I would drive her to San Pedro High School and give her money for lunch; only by accident did I learn I was wasting my time. One day, I came home at noon to retrieve some documents I had forgotten and found Paula at home with her boyfriend, that I didn't know she had! She freaked. I was fried. This was not good.

Having learned a great deal about life or so I thought, I mistakenly believed I was ready to manage just about any family situation, but nothing had prepared me for this scenario. Buscaglia had taught me about beauty and joy and spirituality and the wonderment of life, but how would I deal with deceit, untruthfulness, and worst of all hopelessness in a young girl? In thought, I realized that I could not control Paula or live her life for her;

I could only point her in the right direction, be always supportive and pray for the best. What I hadn't understood was that her behavior and personality had already molded.

Paula, I learned, had not attended school at all after her first day. After I would drop her off in the morning, she would just casually walk home. Her next stop on the way to reaching the age of majority (not maturing) was my dad's place in Baldwin Park where she would attend a church school. Her grandparents were good for her, and we all hoped for the best. What we discovered, to our dismay, was that Paula had finely honed her lying and deception skills, and she became proficient at not telling the truth. Unknowingly, she was doing herself a great disfavor. She was untruthful, always evasive, and heading in a very dangerous direction. The situation was difficult for all of us involved as we never experienced anything like this when we were growing up. We thought Paula may have had a drug problem, but fortunately, that was not the case. She simply had no self-esteem and no confidence.

Meanwhile, at the courthouse, Judge Biggerstaff had spent his time in the barrel and was reassigned to a department where he would oversee Probate cases, as well as discovery motions on pending civil litigation. He had a new research attorney (law clerk) assigned to him named Julie. She was enthusiastic about her job; she was brilliant and talked in 75¢ words. Julie had graduated near the top of her law school class. Engaging in conversation with her was an enjoyable pleasure and I admired her always polite, sophisticated manner and charming personality. There were times, however, when Julie didn't seem very happy at all, but I figured it was a female thing or, perhaps, just mood swings. I had no idea of the unhappiness in her life as she hid her true feelings very well. So when a group of us from the courthouse planned a weekend skiing trip to June Mountain on a 3-day weekend, she was invited. "Might cheer you up," I suggested, and told her we had perhaps 15 or 16 people going, including never-on-time Tom.

Trying to convince her to let loose and enjoy herself, I jokingly told her Tom was a real character who took 20 minutes to fix a salad that was already made and she laughed. Julie said she would love to go, but she was having marital difficulties and was trying to work them out. When

I returned to work on Tuesday, Monday was a holiday, our bailiff told me Julie had a severe case of lead poisoning over the weekend and would not be returning to work. Bailiff's have a warped sense of humor. Julie's estranged husband had shot her and himself, a murder suicide that was on the news for days.

Judge Biggerstaff was without a research attorney and had the judicial secretary schedule interviews for a new law clerk. One of the interviewees came in one afternoon looking a little unsure of herself. Not knowing she was there to interview, I pleasantly asked I if could help her. She must have thought I was a little weird as I was listening to country music and reading the newspaper in the courtroom. She introduced herself as Mary Anne Morrison and she was there to interview with Judge Biggerstaff. The rest is history, so to speak.

Several months passed and I was living leisurely in Palos Verdes, too far to ride a bicycle to work, but not too far for a motorcycle. My La Mans Centurion had been replaced with the Rolls Royce of bicycles: a Colnago, an Italian racing machine. I had it built at King's Bicycle Shop in San Pedro. I also had a Kawasaki 550 (black with green striping) with a belt drive. Prior to that I had a Kawasaki 440, also a nice quiet ride and I had many pleasurable experiences just riding. Some of those involved Chris when he was 4, sitting in front of me on the gas tank as we rode down the street. The Kawasaki was fairly quiet for a motorcycle and real easy on petrol.

Since I was in closer proximity to my computer buddies, my education was heading in a new direction. Although I had yet to realize it, a new adventure with profit was on the horizon, a great deal of profit. In a very short time, I would turn my computer hobby into a money-making business that would make my life a blur for years and leave me wondering where it all went (time & money). The unfortunate thing about making a great deal of money is that it doesn't guarantee happiness, and most often it is accompanied with emotional emptiness. Don't get me wrong, I loved the income, but not the distress that came with it.

Kawasaki

Chapter 28: Computers

Early in 1982, I gave a great deal of thought about the future, not mine, but my son's. With automation starting to evolve at a quicker pace, I decided to buy a computer to give him a head start, and I thought it might be fun, too. People were saying that computers were the thing of the future. How wrong they were. Computers were the thing of the present, but most folks didn't realize it yet. Apple, Amiga, Commodore, and TRS (Texas-Instruments) were the current main choices. IBM would soon be bringing out the PC, but the price would be outrageous. A very good book called "Accidental Empires" tells terrific stories about automation, computers, and the people being in the right place at the right time, Bill Gates in particular.

I bought an Apple IIE computer system and excitedly brought it home. I made all the connections and when I was ready, I turned it on, only to look at a blank screen! The darn thing wouldn't work or so I thought. Actually, it worked just fine. All it needed was software, but I had no software for the stupid thing. I quickly learned that software was expensive and didn't come with the computer. More than that, it cost money and I didn't care for that part of the bargain at all and set out to acquire as much of it as possible with no cost involved. I bought a couple of games and books. The first game I bought was called Load-Runner and I played that marvelous, little silly game for hours. The first night I kept playing and playing and playing and soon the sun was coming up and I had to go to work. Dumb ! ! !

The books I purchased dealt with the BASIC programming language and provided me an insight to what computers could do, now and in the future. I taught myself, as best I could, how to write simple programs. I joined a computer club made up of folks who owned Apple computers where I was to meet Ernie Neagle and Tom Murphy. Ernie was an engineer who worked for Hughes Aircraft in El Segundo, California, while Tom was a computer analyst/tech who worked for McDonnell-Douglas in Long Beach. Ernie was a little genius who was excellent at cracking software and over the next couple years passed his knowledge on to me. I learned 'Assembler' which was one of the main Apple software gaming languages at the time. Tom Murphy was an eccentric who looked very much like a lumberjack, short and stocky with a heavy beard, but had the manners of a much gentler person, and he was extremely polite. I observed him a great deal and assimilated part of his manner into my own. At one of our monthly computer club meetings, Tom gave a lecture entitled, "How Data Travels." Tom was a superb programmer and later in 1984, he would assume an intricate role in computer operations at McDonnell-Douglas as that was the main center for broadcasting the 1984 Olympics from Los Angeles. After a few years of membership in the Pirates Bay computer club, I had almost every piece of software available for the Apple IIE on 5¼" diskettes. 3½" diskettes weren't around yet and I had no idea what a hard drive was, never heard of one.

One afternoon while lounging around at his house, Ernie spoke of building an IBM clone after acquiring the individual parts over time. The IBM PC cost well over $5000 and no one I knew had one or could afford one. Tidbit you may find interesting: The term "PC" was 'trademarked' by IBM so no other manufacture could use it. Every computer sold would be a "clone" except for the IBM; it would be the PC (personal computer). Ernie and I started buying parts and stashing them away while I still lived in West Covina. By the time I had moved to Palos Verdes, we both had all the parts necessary and one Saturday afternoon in the summer of 1986, I started assembling my first clone computer. It worked! Guess what? No software. Sound familiar? So we started the process of acquiring different versions of DOS and utility software through computer club contacts and we were fairly successful at it.

By the mid-eighties I was heavily involved with computers and spent most of my free time learning everything I could about them. By the end of 1986, the IBM PC was the hottest thing going, but they were out to lunch on their prices. I started buying parts and assembling IBM clones and selling them to make a small profit. I won't go into detail, but getting computers to function properly in the 80s was a dreadful task. Things got better when the IDE (Integrated Drive Electronics) controllers and drives hit the market. Prior to that, hard drives had to be processed or "debugged" using DOS for low-level formatting preparation. Only after a drive was debugged could it be partitioned and then formatted, quite a list of tasks and they all had to be done sequentially and correctly. I'm getting a little carried away here, but this was the start of a hobby that eventually turned very profitable.

Mary Anne and I started dating in 1986 and our relationship progressed quickly, perhaps a little too quickly. We enjoyed each other's company and she was a bright, intelligent lady. In retrospect, there were bright red, glowing neon warning signs that I buzzed through like a blind person on a road course. She mentioned on a number of occasions that she was shy of speaking in front of people and had joined Toastmasters to acquire better speaking skills; she needed the exposure to feel more at ease when arguing a case in court. She would never be very good at it, though. Eventually, she and I would discuss a deeper relationship, but there was problem. I had a young son that I wanted to live with me, with us. Mary Anne would have nothing to do with that (warning sign #1). She was adamant that our relationship could not have the interference of "an instant family" (warning sign #2). She made it clear that my son, Chris, would not be welcome (warning sign #3). Then, because she was an attorney and I was just a lowly court clerk, she wanted a written pre-nuptial agreement (warning sign #4), because, after all she would always make more money than me (that never happened). Stupid Steven had been alone too long and just didn't see, or didn't want to see, the warning signs. I relented (my mistake, Chris, I apologize) and we were married in September 1988 at the Wayfarer's Chapel in Palos Verdes. My best man was also my best friend, Doug McKee, the Supervising Judge in the Torrance Court.

I owned a beautiful townhouse in Rancho Palos Verdes and as soon as we were married, I quit-claimed it to both Mary Anne and me. I gave half the value of my home to my new wife and I did so freely. Sharing was a natural part of my personality, but not my wife's. Mary Anne was not the sharing kind (warning sign #5) and in time that fact would eventually doom our marriage. For an intelligent guy, I have had absolutely no luck with relationships and I don't blame anyone but myself. I shouldn't sound so bleak, because she and I traveled a great deal and enjoyed life to its fullest for a few years anyway. Time passed very quickly as I became more and more involved in the IT field. Sure, I had built and sold many computers over the past few years, but that was nothing in comparison to what would soon happen.

I had always been generous, sometimes to a fault. That hasn't changed much even later in life. But the manner in which I got that way is an interesting and personally touching story.

It was a hot, muggy July afternoon in 1968 with the temperature in the 90s and I was driving to LAX to drop off a young lady who was flying to Oakland or San Francisco that afternoon, I don't remember which one. What I do remember, quite clearly, is that I was flat broke. Without a job, I had borrowed $5 for gas from a friend and had no way to pay it back as I was in one of my "down periods" where things were not going so well. I had enough gas to get to the airport, but the return trip would be very 'iffy' if you know what I mean. In any event, I also didn't have the money to pay for airport parking so I found a spot several blocks from the airport entrance and the two of us walked the half mile or so to the terminal. It was a sad parting and I wish to this day that I hadn't let her board that plane, but I did so silently. I walked back to my car in a dismal state of mind still realizing that I probably would not make it the 50 miles home. When I got to my car and started the engine, there in the crease of the glove-compartment was wedged a twenty dollar bill. That sweet girl who left on the plane had stuck it there knowing my plight, and the remarkable thing about it was she didn't have the money either, but she gave it anyway. It was one of the purest and simplest lessons I have ever learned and I have given freely my entire life because of it.

Chapter 29: Novell Networks

When Judge Biggerstaff announced his retirement in 1986, the door opened for my ride up the management ladder. I had fulfilled my commitment to him and anxiously looked forward to expanding my knowledge and my career. But more importantly, I would have an opportunity to make a difference for others. First though, I was again sent around the county to substitute for other court clerks who were on vacation. One of my assignments was to Judge Douglas A. McKee in Torrance for a death penalty retrial on a case that Chief Justice Rose Bird had overturned. Of the 64 death penalty cases she reviewed, Rose Bird had overturned all 64 of them. The California voters would shortly remove her from the bench. My assignment on that retrial would last nearly two months with hundreds of exhibits. Because the courts were not yet computerized, except for downtown Los Angeles, I brought my computer to the courtroom and indexed the entire trial proceedings and tracked every trial exhibit on it. Doug and I became good friends and I learned he was president of the Palos Verdes Little League. I met his wife, Sheila (he nicknamed her "Mouse") and his two sons, Drake and Grant. Soon thereafter I offered a little baseball assistance that I knew the kids would enjoy. I computerized the Palos Verdes Little League stats. I provided printouts showing each player's batting statistics (average, at bats, hits, runs, RBIs and even pitcher's ERA). Every Saturday morning the postings would be surrounded by little leaguers looking at their numbers which gave me a great deal of enjoyment and satisfaction.

Doug McKee was quite a handsome man with a warm and friendly personality, and a very popular judge; he was leading the perfect life. He lived in Rolling Hills Estates, had a beautiful wife and two wonderful boys. During the retrial in his court, he would continually apologize to the jury for any inconvenience and there were many as the trial lasted nearly two months. At the conclusion of the trial the jurors presented him with a needle-point that said "I Apologize" on it, a very cute and kind gesture.

I moved into management with the Superior Court later in 1986 and was assigned to the Central District downtown. The Superior Court was in the process of computerizing operations and there was not a great deal of internal talent available. From the judges who knew me, I stood out like a sore thumb. Soon I set up training classes for the judiciary in downtown LA. The success of those training classes and my reputation spread quickly throughout the court and put another event into motion that would benefit both the court and me. I was asked to take my training classes on the road and to include courtroom clerks and managers. For nearly two years I would travel from district to district and put on training classes from 5:00—7:00 p.m. most nights, and I did it on my own time without compensation. Let me put this into proper perspective. The Los Angeles Superior Court is the largest judicial system in the world! There are 52 separate court locations with more than 650 judges! For a short time I was encased as the only non-judicial member of the Superior Court Automation Committee. In discussions with vendors and state agencies, I asked pointed questions and the committee pretty much gave me free reign. They trusted me and I didn't let them down. I was very fortunate to have had the opportunity to assist in setting standards for our court and the California Judicial Council adopted most of the standards I developed in Los Angeles, although those have changed over the years.

At my request, the court sent me to Novell for network training. The present network system in the court, Banyan Vines, was not conducive to all areas of litigation and overly expensive to operate. Novell would be the replacement platform. The training was expensive (for the court) and thorough, taking me nearly two months to acquire my certificate. I was the first Novell CNA (Certified Netware Administrator) in the court; unfortunately, I would not have the opportunity to use those skills with the Superior Court, but I would use them. Boy, would I use them.

Mary Anne was employed by the law firm of Liebman, Reiner & McNeil in downtown Los Angeles. That firm had a few computers, but no network. One day, Mary Anne called me at the courthouse and asked if I would come by her law firm after work. They had a couple of computers that didn't work properly and Mary Anne had mentioned that I might be able to assist them. The firm had a computer tech on call, but he wasn't reliable and could not fix the present problems. After spending about an hour repairing the computers to where they functioned better than before, the office manager, Helen, told me to submit an invoice. "For what?" I asked her. She gave me a peculiar look and I told her it was a pleasure helping my wife's firm and that there would be no invoice. Then Helen asked me if I would be interested in a retainer to fix their computers, say $500 a month. Of course I would and when the opportunity presented itself, and it did, I made a suggestion to Stuart Liebman, the managing partner, that he could increase productivity a hundred fold if the Liebman firm had a computer network where the secretaries could share files, not just in the L.A. office, but in all seven of their offices statewide. The secretaries' greatest contribution was typing legal documents and by sharing those files on a network, a tremendous amount of time could be saved. Stuart was interested, but I was not so bold as to make the presentation.

While attending the Novell classes, I met Nicole Merry who spoke with a silver tongue and knew everything about Novell networks. I asked Nicole if she would make the presentation and she said she would, for $200 now and $300 more if they bought it. I didn't have $200 and so I made her an offer she couldn't refuse. I said, "Nicole, if you're as good as you say you are, this will be a slam-dunk. Tell you what, I'll give you 1/3 of the profit from the network installation if you can sell it to Liebman." She agreed. Her network presentation was flawless and Liebman bought it hook, line and sinker. Liebman's decision to install Novell networks in all his locations meant a great deal of money for me, but more importantly, it meant an incredible increase in his firm's productivity.

I had a partner named Hector Aizcorbe (from Argentina) who worked for Nissan. Over the next weekend, he and I installed our first Novell network in the Liebman office in downtown Los Angeles. When the check rolled in, I called Nicole and invited her for dinner where I gave her a cashier's check for $5000 and thanked her no end. She was shocked and surprised and said she would always be available to do it again anytime, but Steven paid close attention and would make all future presentations himself . . .

Interlude . . .

I'll venture that you both find all this stuff a bit much to digest. After all, it does sound a bit far-fetched, perhaps like James Thurber's Walter Mitty, the ineffectual dreamer, but it's all true. Chris will remember some parts; Alicia won't as she wasn't here yet. Admittedly, your dad has a way of expanding things, but it's my story, no one else's; so it's okay. I still remember my mom telling me I would always be a dreamer . . .

On the lighter side, there are some things I lived through that I wish both of you could experience; unfortunately you cannot. First and foremost, I grew up in a much simpler time where people actually enjoyed each other and were much friendlier than they are today, i.e. Ozzie & Harriet and Father Knows Best. Life then was unhurried and uncluttered from all the electronic gadgets that block the view of life. Believe it or not, there were no freeways (except for the one in Pasadena, the first one in the world). Unlike today, it seemed that no one was in a hurry. In the present day, people can't get out of each other's way fast enough and because of that life is a blur; tomorrow is just like yesterday. No one stops to smell the roses; everyone is so damn serious. That's sad, but it doesn't have to be.

IMHO, I grew up in the best of times. Before my generation, life was a great deal tougher because of World Wars I & II and the Great Depression. By the 1950s, things had pretty much settled down and remained that way for quite a few years, my youthful years. Then came the turbulent 1960s with the civil rights movement, Viet Nam, and political unrest. Changes were taking place and many of them were questionable. For the next generation, Chris's generation, moral values, integrity, and discipline have deteriorated to an unhealthy level where in schools some teachers are afraid to teach. The confrontation from students and parents alike is a tremendous incentive for teachers to leave their chosen profession. It was never that way when I was a child. Back then kids respected and honored teachers, and accepted discipline when it was warranted; I should know as I warranted a great deal of it. From my perspective, society is in big trouble, and corruption is rampant everywhere. Wow! Doesn't sound good, does it?

In my younger days, there were no electronics to temp, misguide and mislead youth. When you learned something, it started with the basics. There were no calculators or computers, no word processors and no spell checkers. The younger generation of today is captivated and enthralled by electronics and are not nearly as healthy as their prior generations. Obesity is everywhere for many reasons, but mainly because it takes no effort to do anything. Little work, even less exercise, and fast foods paint a bleak future for the youth of today. Further, society is blighted by drugs, violence, moral decay, political deception, and the disturbingly apparent lack of interest in education. George Orwell wrote 1984 for the wrong period in time; big brother has arrived. We're now in the 21st century where everyone spies on everyone else. Some will argue that's how it should be, where no one gets away with anything. That cost, however, may be too great to pay in a free society. Oops! That's another slam on our too liberal society, isn't it? Sorry.

Secondly, I lived through the emergence of computers in everyday life and I was fortunate enough to make a fairly substantial income from it, although none of it remains. It was fun while it lasted, though. Today's generation, however, takes it all for granted. I know you are both guilty of that and I find that fact more than a little unnerving. You "could" run out and get the latest and greatest of just about anything electronic (Chris does) without really thinking if you "should." The 'now' generation is suffering from delusional self-entitlement and is keenly listening to the WIIFM (What's In It For Me) radio station.

On pleasant reflection, I enjoyed the evolution of many things you two don't give a second thought to: jet travel, colored television, calculators, microwave ovens, chrome rims, wireless phones, computers, 4 & 8 track tape decks (pre-cassette and CDs), Beta and VHS video (before DVDs), space exploration, and cable TV. Chris would probably add creation of the automobile, but I'm not quite that old. What I'm saying is that life was fun and uncomplicated. Heck, you could buy a new house in the 1960s for under $20,000. Try buying a car for that amount these days.

I am coming to a part in my story where the years are blurred together, mostly because I was as guilty then as you are now. I was in too much of a hurry. I was caught up in the rat race and I'll admit that I felt bullet-proof like most young people. How wrong I was. Oh, I was a charmer and could sell a computer to a monkey, but life just sort of got away from me. I neglected my family for the almighty dollar. What a waste. I created a corporation called "LegalTech" where I sold and serviced computers to judges and sold networks to law firms and dental offices around the state. If I had it to do over again, I wouldn't. Instead of chasing the dollar, I should have endeavored to do what Thomas Jefferson so eloquently wrote in the Declaration of Independence: the pursuit of happiness.

For most of us, being happy starts with having enough income to do what you want and buy what you want: a nice home, food, clothes, car, and pleasurable activities and vacations, of course, all within reason. But happiness is much more than that. It's more than just having enough money and it's much more that having lots of stuff. It's being healthy, free from pain, being able to take care of oneself, and having good times with friends and family. Further, happiness means being able to speak what's on your mind without fear of retribution, to worship the God of your choosing, and to feel safe and secure in your own home. It means having the opportunity to get an education, to be an entrepreneur, and to pursue your dreams. That's the big one, kids, pursuing your dreams. If you have no dreams, you'll have no life.

There are three things I now have in my life that you should always have: hope, peace, and honesty. It wasn't always that way, and it took a great deal of sacrifice to get here, but I am enjoying every single day as it comes. Every day is beautiful in its own way. Remember, I'm on borrowed time . . .

. . . back to reality.

Chapter 30: Opportunity

While working in the Central District Courthouse in downtown Los Angeles, I would be summoned from time to time by various judges for assistance with their computers and some of those encounters were simply hilarious. I remember telling one of the judges that his computer might just work a little better if it had electricity. We both chuckled at that remark.

One of those judges was Ricardo Torres who would become the Presiding Judge for the entire court in January 1990. Rick and I became good friends and golf buddies and I serviced his computer at home, always at no charge. I met his kids (all adults) who became like family to me. One of his sons, Ricardo Jr., was an attorney who operated a free legal clinic for the poor and destitute folks who could not afford to hire an attorney. I computerized his legal clinic at no cost and RT2, as he was called, would later assist me in my legal squabbles with Mary Anne. It's amazing what friends will actually do for each other when there is a true need. Further, I donated and serviced two computers and HP LaserJet printers during RT2's unsuccessful bid for a seat on the Los Angeles City Council. Michael Torres, another of Rick's sons, was a real character with a hilarious personality – always beaming a bright smile. He worked for the Interpreter's Office in the Superior Court. I hired him to assist me in network installations and service.

Because of my friendship with the presiding judge, I was soon "given" an assignment that I didn't want any part of doing. When first presented with the opportunity as it was called by Ray Arce from upper court management, I politely turned it down. The assignment was a project to clean up and rearrange the court's file room operations that housed more than 3 million court files. Ray was persistent and told me it was a golden opportunity to make a name for myself and help the court. I thanked him again and said it wasn't my specialty and that I knew nothing about file room operations. Later that afternoon Ricardo Torres summoned me to his chambers. His secretary, Gloria, smiled as I entered and said, "He's waiting for you," and winked as if she already knew what was going to happen. When I entered his chambers, Rick was eased back in his leather chair and said, "I told Ray to give you that assignment. The file room downstairs is a disaster and I need it cleaned up. Court files are lost and misplaced, and important documents are nowhere to be found. And I need someone down there I can trust. Now, go back and tell him you changed your mind." Well, I did as I was told, didn't really have a choice.

In hindsight, Rick was right. The file room was a disaster. Court files were stacked 3 or 4 feet high in the isles and on carts. There was not enough room on the shelves for them. There were literally thousands of court documents in bundled stacks that had not been filed away, and when files were needed in the courtroom, they often times could not be found. When they were found, they were usually incomplete which caused a great deal of dismay, confusion and anger from the bench. There were approximately 500,000 case files in the file room for probate, civil and family law cases, and another 3 million files in the court archives across the street. Moreover, the attitude of the employees was pathetic and most of them moped around in a dazed manner as if lost. They had no motivation and no hope; some were just bad news. They were now my responsibility and I was given to the end of May (2 months) to clean it up, a seemingly impossible situation in everyone's eyes.

Since I was given complete autonomy for this assignment (Rick had plowed the road), I took a very proactive and aggressive approach to it. Very recently, a new courthouse had been opened, also in downtown Los Angeles. It was called Central Civil West (CCW) and was just a couple miles away. Since it was a new facility, there was plenty of storage space so I used part of my staff and the court facilities services to move thousands of court files to CCW. The files I had moved were ones where the case was closed. I had those files charted and indexed so any file could be located when needed. There were seasoned employees in the file room who knew just about everything about file operations who had been passed over or just pushed aside by others eager to prove their moxie to court management. Well, Steven is no dummy and I made it a point to personally interview each and every member of my new staff and I found my "Acres of Diamonds" right where I knew they would be. Part of my education with Buscaglia was the direction he persuaded me to go. He pointed me to Russell Conwell.

What I discovered from discussions with the employees was a picture of an operation that had no chance of succeeding. Morale was an unknown word and because of past treatment, employees went through the motions but didn't really do what was expected of them, at least not from my viewpoint. I interviewed prospective new employees with a single goal in mind: to instill pride in the staff and present opportunities to anyone who wanted to succeed. So, I'll tell you a story about Jessica, Mary, Greg, and Steve.

During Jessica's interview, I learned she was a single mother and had been an aerobics instructor, but had injured herself and could no longer perform. She had a young daughter and desperately needed a job to support her family. But the most significant aspect of Jessica was her seemingly boundless energy, beautiful smile, and very open personality. She was friendly and presented a warm and positive attitude. I needed that attitude.

Mary was a different type of interview. She had graduated from U.S.C. and had worked as an office manager prior to suffering a tragic automobile accident that nearly killed her and left her with a very noticeable limp and an outwardly altered appearance. Additionally, she had difficulty speaking. Because of her accident, Mary could no longer perform in her previous profession and was relegated to finding employment where she was over-qualified. More than two years had passed since her accident and she had interviewed with the County of Los Angeles on nine previous occasions without success. At the conclusion of her interview I asked her if there was anything she would like to add that would enhance her possibility of acquiring one of the open positions. It took her more than a minute to quietly gather her thoughts and slowly, painfully tell me, "Mr. Forrest. I hope my disability won't hamper me from getting a job." I sat back in my chair for a moment and then looked her straight in the eye and responded, "Mary, I wasn't aware that you had a disability." She started to cry; then she smiled openly and thanked me for the interview. She had brightened my day. Mary clearly possessed organizational skills that others didn't uncover simply because they couldn't see past her appearance.

My interview with Greg was like pulling teeth. Greg was a Native American Indian who had also unsuccessfully interviewed several times. Did he have an educational background? No. Was he motivated? Couldn't really tell at the time. Did he possess any marketable skills that would benefit my operation? Probably not. But there was something about him that caught my attention. Although he didn't appear confident (he wasn't), he was proud of his heritage and proud he was off of the reservation. What I sensed about Greg was loyalty.

There are many other stories likes Jessica's, Mary's & Greg's. It took a week of long interviews and when completed, I had a staff that would have made Nordstrom's envious. They were outgoing, friendly, helpful and best of all, they would become a team. Since I knew little about file room operations, I used those fine folks who had been passed over or just shuffled aside to train and supervise the new staff. There was a lot of hard work to be done and a mission to accomplish, and yet it was becoming fun; moreover, it was an enjoyable challenge.

I had been given complete authority to get the job done and on the last day of May the executive officer, James Dempsey, walked speechlessly around the file room at 7:00 a.m., up and down every isle to see every file in its place and the floor cleaned and polished. The place just sparkled. "No one expected you to do this, Steve. Congratulations," he said and then left. The employees cheered for themselves. They deserved it.

A great deal of help and assistance with this project was given to me by my employees, especially from one of the most popular and loudest members of my staff. His name was Steve Franklin and I had been given a suggestive directive to fire him from one of the judges. What I have forgotten to mention is that I had to eliminate the problem employees while simultaneously performing my assignment. Judge Cardenas had informed me that Mr. Franklin was a big problem and should be terminated. I was informed by Human Resources (HR) that it was nearly impossible to fire a permanent employee without cause and I guess it was (past tense). I fired 29 people in the first two weeks. My new nickname in the court was, "the terminator." When HR management informed me of the proper protocol to follow, I ignored them and said they should complain to the presiding judge, my decisions stood. Didn't win any points there, did I? Didn't care, either.

During my interview with Steve Franklin, I learned he had three kids and was struggling with keeping his family together. His wife, Tara, also worked for me in the Exhibits Room. I knew from observation that Mr. Franklin was a natural leader and the good employees respected him. When I told Mr. Franklin that Judge Cardenas wanted me to fire him, he became very docile and asked if I could transfer him instead to the Compton Court. "Can't do it, Steve," I told him pointedly. "But I'll make you an offer. I really need your assistance here. You help me with this project and if we're successful, I'll have you transferred to Compton on June 1st. If we don't succeed, you're gone. Simple as that. We'll work 7 days a week to get it done. Interested?" He asked if I would be there with him 7 days a week. I nodded and said I would buy the donuts. On June 1st Steve Franklin was transferred to the Compton Court. Opportunity works both ways and Leo Buscaglia would have been proud of his unknown protégé.

Because of my success in doing a task considered to be impossible, I was promoted to district manager (Administrator) and didn't even know it. I hadn't even taken the exam as I was not yet qualified with time in grade. My next pay check was several hundred dollars more than usual and when I inquired in Human Resources to the reason, I was given the news. My promotion was ordered by Ricardo Torres. (Thanks, Rick!)

I mentioned the phrase "Acres Of Diamonds" for a personal reason. I had read Russell H. Conwell's book years before as recommended to me by Leo Buscaglia. "Acres of Diamonds" originated as a speech which Conwell delivered over 6,000 times around the world. It was first published in 1890 by the John Y. Huber Company of Philadelphia, and Conwell used the income from his speeches to found Temple University so that the poor and downtrodden of Philadelphia could attend a school of higher education which otherwise would be out of reach for them.

Russell Herman Conwell (February 15, 1843 – December 6, 1925) was an American Baptist minister, orator, philanthropist, lawyer, and writer. He is best remembered as the founder and first president of Temple University in Philadelphia, and for his inspirational lecture **Acres of Diamonds**. He was born in South Worthington, Massachusetts, and is buried in the Founder's Garden at Temple University.

Interesting fact on Conwell: Jeremiah McCarthy was a young Irish immigrant who had falsified his age to become a Union soldier and fight for America. He was just shy of his 18th birthday when Captain Conwell saved his life. In the morning following Pickett's Charge at Gettysburg, when the smoke had cleared, Conwell discovered Pvt. McCarthy's bloody body lying among the dead soldiers on the fields of Gettysburg. The two had known each other for some time prior and had grown fairly close; this may be why Conwell stopped and knelt down next to Jeremiah (to bid him farewell). Captain Conwell realized that Private McCarthy was still breathing, that he was still alive. With a heartbeat, a blood-stained uniform and a gaping bullet wound in his right forehead, McCarthy was lifted onto Conwell's horse and was taken back to get medical care. He went on to live a long prosperous life and always credited Conwell with giving him the *opportunity* to live past his 18th year and well into his 70s when he died.

The central idea of Conwell's work is that one need not look elsewhere for opportunity, achievement, or fortune—the resources to achieve all good things are present in one's own community. This theme is developed by an introductory anecdote, told to Conwell by an Arab guide, about a man who wanted to find diamonds so badly that he sold his farm and went off in a futile search across Africa to find them. Meanwhile, the new owner of his farm discovered a stone in a creek one day that gave off light in a remarkable manner. The farm was literally covered in "acres of diamonds" that the farmer had failed to look for there. His farm was located above the richest diamond mine on the continent and the farmer had simply walked away from it. Conwell elaborates on the theme through examples of success, genius, service, or other virtues involving ordinary Americans contemporary to his audience: "dig in your own back-yard!" Russell H. Conwell is one of my heroes.

Opportunity is one of three things in life that, once gone, rarely comes back. The others are time and words. I was so incredibly fortunate to have someone like Ricardo Torres push me into the best opportunity in my career. Although I had leadership qualities, without Rick pushing me, they may never have surfaced the way they did, and I cannot say how much I respected that man. Using the wrong words at the wrong time can kill an opportunity. Used in the proper combination, time, words and opportunity can have a significant impact on your future. Carpe diem !

Chapter 31: The Hit Man

You are both aware that your dad has a very fairly strong personality and is not easily discouraged, and, in fact, enjoys a scrappy challenge every now and then. Because of others, I was fortunate with my achievement in the Central District File Room, but with that success came a continual rocky road of challenges in a dual-court environment that many actually wanted to see fail.

By legislative mandate, the Superior Courts and the Municipal Courts were merging throughout California. The superior court judges, without acknowledging it publicly, looked down on the municipal court judges as "underlings" who managed traffic cases and misdemeanor trials while the superior court judges performed the meat and potatoes of judicial work: probate estates, felony trials (murder, robbery, rape, fraud), and civil litigation where the awards could reach into the millions of dollars. With the merger, the municipal court judges would receive a de facto elevation (without appointment) to the superior court bench and receive a huge raise in pay. Although the municipal court judges would have to give up autonomy, the rise in stature was well worth the price. So the battle began.

There were several municipal courts in Los Angeles County that were run by head-strong administrators that superior court management wanted controlled. Ricardo Torres stepped in again, through the Assistant Executive Officer, Johnny Johnson, and I was reassigned to the Torrance Court as the Superior Court District Manager (Administrator) in 1992. My assignment there was no fluke; I was to dislodge control of the courthouse away from municipal court management. The municipal court administrator, Christopher Crawford, was a real piece of work and the Superior Court Administrator, Lynn Seabury, a longtime friend of mine, was an incredibly bright man, but non-confrontational. Most importantly, Doug McKee had been elevated to Supervising Judge of the Torrance Court. Although he had been in power for several years in the South Bay Municipal Court, Chris Crawford didn't have a chance.

Unification meetings were held with the three court locations in my district: Torrance Superior Court, Inglewood Municipal Court, and South Bay Municipal Court. The objective of these meetings was to find common ground so that when the courts merged as directed by legislation, employees could be used in the most efficient and effective manner to achieve a cohesive and disciplined work force. There was a great deal of huffing and puffing (hot air) going around the tables as the municipal court managers were a bit uneasy about merging with the superior courts. Contrary to past behavior, I wasn't at all verbose and instead assumed an amiable posture and observed their behavior closely. When appropriate, I led table discussions by realistic examples and not by over-bearing pressure.

I now had my first courthouse to manage and started the way I did with my previous project. I personally interviewed each member of my staff; it became a very astute and useful management tool. I wanted to get to know them on a personal level. More importantly, I wanted to use my position to enhance the careers of those I found deserving. At every opportunity, I would provide impetus to help others along their career path. To build their self-confidence and a more focused team, I stressed and taught employees 'goal setting' and led by example. I was the first one at work in the morning and usually the last to leave. The superior court seemed to be in a continual vacuum of budget crisis, yearly as I recall. Because of this, I did something most thought was idiotic. I sponsored employees to attend training seminars to strengthen their knowledge and job skills, but more importantly I sent them to build their self-esteem. Sounds good so far, but now I'll tell you about Julie, one of my proudest accomplishments.

Julie was a student worker whose primary function was to sort and distribute mail going to the courtrooms. She was around 25 years old and attended her duties every single day for seven years. Because she was a student worker, she was not entitled to benefits of any kind. No medical, no dental, no vacation. Nothing. A large part of her small income went to pay for medical expenses and, thankfully, she still lived at home.

Julie desired to be hired on a permanent basis and receive the benefits everyone around her took for granted. Unfortunately, there was a problem. Julie was developmentally disabled and had contracted Polio as a child. She was mentally slow, but because she had performed her one job repetitiously over the years, she did it very well. However, it was impossible for her to pass the entrance exam, and she took it every six months for years. She never came close. Her attitude, however, was something to behold. Always warm and friendly, she would greet everyone each morning with a smile. I learned long ago that your attitude will determine your altitude, and so I did something that was not ethically correct. In fact, it was very incorrect. I arranged for Julie to take the entrance exam again, only at the courthouse and not downtown Los Angeles. That was okay, unusual perhaps, but still okay. When the HR tech arrived to administer the 30-minute exam, I put Julie in my office where she received her instruction for the exam. Then I did it. I took the HR tech to lunch. He said Julie only had 30 minutes and I told him not to worry, she wouldn't pass anyway. She didn't.

I received a phone call from HR that afternoon telling me she didn't pass. Of course, I knew she wouldn't pass. She needed to score 25 on the exam to pass. When informed of Julie's failure, all I said to the tech was, "Tell me she got 20." After a few moments of discussion, I was informed that Julie had indeed scored just 20 correct answers on the exam, still not enough for her to be promoted. That's all I needed to hear. Because of my previous dealings with Human Resources downtown, I knew that if someone failed, but scored 80% of the score needed to pass, they could be hired on a probationary basis. So I promoted Julie to a temporary position as an Office Assistant I. In order for her to be hired permanently, she had to perform her duties satisfactorily for six months. Piece of cake. After her probationary period, Julie became a permanent employee and we threw her a party. What I did was wrong, according to the rules. What I did was right, according to my heart. Would I do it again . . . ? In a heartbeat.

There were other opportunities that presented themselves. My Novell training would come into play almost immediately. With a little assistance from the facilities staff from the South Bay Municipal Court, we laid coaxial cable throughout the Superior Court building in Torrance and installed a Novell network at no cost to the court (10Base-T technology was not yet available). The $25,000 cost for that network was borne by me. The court had been very good to me; I was returning the favor.

A little more than a year after my assignment there, Chris Crawford voluntarily left court service and moved to northern California where he started a successful lecture business. Chris and I actually became friends and I confided in him that because of his past clashes with the Board of Supervisors, his future didn't bode well with the courts. He wasn't quite sure whether to believe me until I did something for him. The municipal court wanted to throw a Christmas party at a local club where the younger generation would hang-out and party, but was denied access. I told Chris I could get it for them and he said, "Yeah, right!" What he didn't know (and I didn't tell him) was that the owner of the establishment was a neighbor of mine in Palos Verdes and we were both on the homeowner's association board of directors. I was board president and my very egotistical neighbor (also named Chris) was the vice-president who wanted my spot. I had been the board president for 3 years and was ready to leave it anyway so I told Chris I would resign and the presidency would be his. All he had to do was allow the Christmas party to go forward at his club. Presto! Chris Crawford was amazed and asked if there was anything I couldn't do. "Don't think so," I said to him. Another win-win opportunity had presented itself and I confess I felt a little smug, although I didn't show it outwardly. Life was good (at work anyway).

I mentioned way back in Chapter 17 that I made a bundle at the track and that I wouldn't return to the races again for more than 20 years. Well, January 25, 1992, marked my return in an interesting sort of way. I was drafted by court management to participate in the corporate challenge, a harness race at Los Alamitos Race Course.

The winter harness season was in full bloom and as an attraction to draw more attendees, the track sponsored a corporate challenge each year. It was a fun evening capped by a two-horse match race around the oval. My trusty steed, named Mystical Traveler, trampled my opposition by eight lengths. Hadn't had so much fun in years. To prepare for the race I went to Los Alamitos one afternoon to train with one of the drivers.

STEVE FORREST, LOS ANGELES SUPERIOR COURT, WINNER
"THE CORPORATE CHALLENGE"

LOS ALAMITOS, CA	5/8 MILE PACE-1:23.1	JANUARY 25, 1992

© Photo by Frank

When I sat in the sulky and he handed me the reins, the driver said to me, "You've done this before, I see." Well I hadn't done it before, but I had been around horses for years and I knew how to handle myself. After one practice lap, the driver told me, "You're done. You won't have any problems on the track." I didn't as I had my horse's head against the starting gate as we approached the starting line, grabbed the lead at the start and it was over. Just a cruise around the track.

Chapter 32: My Frightened Children

On the home front, Mary Anne didn't particularly care for the townhouse in Palos Verdes and wanted what she called "a real house" close to the ocean, if possible. Property prices were sky high on the ocean and yet I plunked down $50K to buy a home at 2131 Vallecito Drive in San Pedro, overlooking the ocean with a direct view of Catalina Island from every room. The location was perfect, but the house was a disaster and needed work, lots of work and landscaping. We still owned the townhouse and because the real estate market wasn't very brisk at the time, I made payments on both places for 20 months. Please take notice that "I" made the payments and not "we" made the payments. Mary Anne, I discovered to my dismay, was not into sharing and I was not a happy camper because of that fact. Oh, she would write me a small check each month for what she called expenses, but a rift was starting to brew in me as this was not part of the bargain I had anticipated. Steven, it seemed, had still not learned. There were three checking accounts in our family and Mary Anne did not contribute to any of them. She kept her own, private and separate, bank accounts. It hurts me to say this, but my wife was not a team player, something I had always been, and it frustrated me to no end. I had responsibility for paying all the expenses and I brought that fact to her attention on several occasions. I offered to give her the checking accounts so she could manage the family expenses. She declined.

Over time the rift would become a river and then an ocean too wide to cross, but that was still down the line. Other, more distressful news was on the horizon that I found neither pleasant nor anticipated. The unusual events that happened in my life had made my journey through it a bit tumultuous at times; thankfully, I've always had a positive spirit, even when it didn't always appear that way. Having a challenge, in my mind, was a much more palatable way of looking at life rather than having a bunch of unresolved problems. That part of my personality would provide me great service while enduring a traumatic and life-threatening accident in the winter of 2006 while living in Washington. (Don't Worry Be Happy—Bobby McFerrin)

Although neither of my children lived with me when I was married to Mary Anne, I enjoyed the moments I shared with them. When Paula and Chris would visit periodically, sometimes together sometimes alone, we would go out for lunch or dinner, sometimes for a movie. Our moments together were light and refreshing and, for the most part, they were upbeat. However, not once during their visits did Mary Anne accompany us and she went out of her way to avoid contact with my children. Perhaps without realizing it, Mary Anne left an uneasy mood in the air each time Paula or Chris came over. No, that's bogus; she knew what she was doing (warning sign #647). She was driving a wedge between us where it would either be her or my children and that was a battle she would never win.

One evening I received a telephone call from Paula and she was crying. Penny was flying home (from San Francisco, I believe) that evening and Paula wanted me to come to Ontario and talk with her and Chris. She was extremely upset and in distress.

When I arrived, Paula told me her mom had cancer. Because Penny's flight wouldn't land in Ontario until later that night, I took Paula and Chris to dinner and they (mostly Paula) openly shed their fears and concerns about the future, possibly without their mother. Chris was a bit more reserved yet I could see the uncertainty and bewilderment in his eyes. Without any sugar-coating, but with the kindness and insight only a parent can give, I told them straightforwardly what the possibilities were and how they would be managed, depending on the outcome of Penny's treatment.

When Penny's flight arrived, the four of us sat down and discussed the future and Penny reassured her children that everything would turn out okay, but I could see she was scared. She would receive radiation treatment from the City of Hope Cancer Center in Duarte. Listening to her, it was easy to see that her initial concern was money and she was uneasy about her financial condition. She was broke and broken. On the spot I wrote her a check for enough money to cover all her expenses for a couple months and I saw relief ease across her face. She looked at the check and then at me. She said she couldn't repay me right away and I told her it wasn't necessary. My gesture that evening did something to Penny that I couldn't do in the short time we were married. I touched her heart and it gave us both a warm, comforting feeling. Fortunately and with the grace of God, Penny survived her ordeal. (Rollin' With The Flow—Charlie Rich)

Chapter 33: The Money Pits

Time became a whirlwind as I was involved in remodeling our fractured house on Vallecito, running an ever-growing computer business, and working for the Superior Court. Over the next year, I sank $250K into the Vallecito house and when it was completed, it was a jewel. My relationship with Mary Anne was on the down slide as she had personally picked out everything for the remodel, insisting on the inclusion of a $25,000 purple, blue, & white swirl marble mantle (imported from France) for the fireplace. Basically, I had little input in the remodel or furnishings, an issue that would creep up again in the future. My computer business was a gold mine and I made $15,000 a month just in service contracts, much more with a network installation. One weekend, Hector and I installed a network for a law firm in San Diego and made $40K each. The money was great, but Steven was not in a happy place and inner peace was missing from my life. I needed to get away from Mary Anne, if just to clear my senses.

Paula called one Saturday morning and wanted to talk about something private. She would explain everything at lunch. As we were having lunch at our favorite weekend diner, the Lighthouse Restaurant in San Pedro, Paula broke the news to me that she was pregnant. Initially, I said nothing and just looked at her and listened. She had done what her mother had done and it was probably the most unintelligent thing she would ever do, and she did it intentionally! She told me her girlfriends all had babies and she wanted one, too. I was listening to the immature ramblings of a very foolish girl, not a 22 year old woman, but a girl. She and the father had no intention of getting married. Paula thought she would just have a baby. How idiotic. I asked her how she planned on supporting a child in our ever-changing and always unforgiving society and she couldn't answer. "It's your life, Paula," is all I would say to her. Stupid, stupid girl. (Papa Don't Preach—Madonna)

I had previously acquired a partner in my network business, Hector Aizcorbe, and together we sold and installed a dozen networks in a three year period. Hector was from Argentina and had previously been a programmer for IBM before moving over to Nissan. He had an extensive knowledge of networking and our partnership, in the short term, blossomed and the money rolled in. However, after I discovered Hector's deceitful and dishonest ways of conducting business, his ethics were my major concern, our partnership dissolved as quickly as it had formed. The sad part of the networking business was the time it took to do it; I was in a different city every weekend and I worked at home most nights. There simply was no free time anymore. On the weekends, I'd be off to San Jose, Santa Ana, San Diego, Sacramento, San Francisco, or Ranch Cucamonga. On a few of my trips to San Francisco I'd venture over to Richmond and San Pablo to search for someone long ago lost to me. Once in a while I'd catch a break and the Liebman firm in Los Angeles kept me home for the weekend. I had lots of help and enjoyed the computer business, but the grind was taking a toll on me. I had no life of my own and it was an empty existence.

The summer of 1993 had passed and I was looking for a way out of my relationship with Mary Anne. Her continual "me" attitude and selfishness had worn me down as, once again, I had successfully failed at a personal relationship. Seems I was an expert at it. Not only that, Mary Anne had quit her job at Liebman and took a position as a research attorney for the Superior Court and a big cut in pay. When I mentioned to her that the she should contribute to our marriage, she just said, "Sell more networks." That was cold and I resented it. I had had enough and was ready to start anew when she broke the news that she was pregnant. That was great, but she was the wrong woman. Then she announced she wanted to move to Palos Verdes and she had located a house overlooking the ocean that was nicer than the one we had, if can you believe that, with a much better school district. Mary Anne said she needed $100,000 for a down payment. I should have passed, but I didn't. She didn't have the money, but I did. I resolved to give it my best for the baby to come and that was probably another Steven screw up. I bought a beautiful piece of property, again overlooking the ocean, located at 3212 Seaclaire Drive in Rancho Palos Verdes. Again I made payments on two homes until the house on Vallecito sold, for what was owed on it! Lost a bundle there thanks to Mary Anne. During our divorce proceedings she made a comment that I blamed her for all the financial losses. She was wrong again. I hadn't blamed her at all, I blamed myself.

Chapter 34: Alicia Arrives

Two terrific events came to pass in 1994. First, I was reassigned to the Jury Division. The previous jury administrator had retired and the Presiding Judge, Gary Klausner, directed the new Executive Officer, Ed Kritzman, to install me as the new Administrator of Jury Operations. The superior court and the municipal courts had merged and Jim Dempsey, the Superior Court Executive Officer, had been displaced by Ed Kritzman from the Los Angeles Municipal Court. That was good and bad. Good for the courts, bad for me.

Judge Klausner's most important concern in the court was the state of the jury system; it was his main priority. Gary Klausner and Doug McKee were good friends and when Gary decided to run for the position of Presiding Judge, he solicited Doug to run his campaign. In his previous job in the District Attorney's Office, Doug was a lobbyist in Sacramento for the DA's office and he spoke with a golden tongue. With his experience, he was a natural to run Gary's campaign. Doug called me and over a pizza, in a very persuasive manner, he "told" me I was part of his team. He spent countless hours calling-in favors and making personal contacts across the county. Gary won on the first ballot as a unanimous selection. My placement in the Jury Division was probably Gary's "thank you." While in the Jury Division, I managed to close many holes and implement ideas that had only been talked about for years, and I made a fatal mistake in judgment, later on that, though. I was a good administrator, but I was a far better project manager. Of all my accomplishments with the court, the one I am most proud of was the installation of the Jury Call Center. Discussions had gone on for years and a resolution could not be reached for any number of reasons. It took me just three weeks to put it all together. The biggest hold up was getting authority to sign the contract that would bind it. A quiet, clandestine discussion with the new "Assistant" Executive Officer, Jim Dempsey, did the trick. But that was not the best thing that happened in '94.

On August 25, 1994, Alicia Lynn Forrest crashed into this world kicking and screaming. I was in the delivery room when she was born and her dad was the first person to greet her as the nurse hoisted her into the world. She was purple! (But only for a short while.) When the nurse cleaned her off and placed her on her mother's stomach, she was quite the prize. There are always details for new-born kidletts that are carried out by the hospital staff. Well, I was going to make sure there were no screw-ups. There would be no chance my new daughter would be switched or have some other malfunction in the system affect her. Like a man possessed, I insisted on being with Alicia for every test and every procedure that was done to her. I went into the nursery and anywhere else they took her: for foot-printing, blood work, pictures, anything at all. When the nurse poked a needle in the bottom of left her foot to get a blood sample for blood-typing, baby Alicia started to cry, but halted her tears as she held my little finger in her tiny hand. She gripped my finger with her left hand and looked in my eyes as if seeking reassurance and I gladly gave it to her. I didn't let her out of my sight. She was a precious cargo, just as Chris had been. Only this time, I would be a better parent. I was and I am, but the future would not be easy for either of us. The time I spent with Alicia while she was a baby is still fresh in my mind. I would carry her around, swinging her and singing Baby Blue (The Echoes) to her. She was the cutest baby alive and she was always laughing and I felt—no, I knew—she had my personality. Later, when it came time for her to start walking, she did something I had never before seen. She was sitting in the middle of the living room and she just stood up with nothing to hold on to or support her. She just stood up. It cracked me up. Then she would sit and start giggling uncontrollably because of her new conquest. Then stand up again. Amazing! We had a round table in our living room and Alicia would chase me around it, laughing as she went.

When Alicia was born, we were in a new home in Palos Verdes. Mary Anne had wanted to move from our hill-side home in San Pedro to Palos Verdes so that Alicia would be in a better school district, even though that was years away. Things don't always turn out as planned . . .

Chapter 35: Magna Carta (History Lesson)

Time for a little break from personal descriptions to describe my more enlightened sense of pride. I am taking this opportunity to offer you two a little of our country's history and some of the events that shaped it; something rarely done by parents anymore, or schools for that matter. Whenever I've had an assignment or a job-related task to perform, my best effort went forward, and so it will here. After all, my philosophy is simple. If something is worth doing, it's worth doing well (not original, I know). So my departure here is simply because the events I'll describe meant a great deal to me personally as I learned them and, after all, it's my story isn't it?

My reassignment to jury operations presented an opportunity to change the outlook most people have about serving on jury duty. Almost unanimously, I discovered, citizens want nothing to do with serving jury duty in any capacity. That's incredibly selfish and disturbing to me since serving on jury duty is the "only" way people can participate directly in their government. While talking to jurors over the years I've learned that citizens believe they live in a democracy in this country. That's hogwash as Buscaglia would say. All anyone has to do is recite the "Pledge of Allegiance" and the answer is blatantly clear. So I thought I would delve into the history of jury service, and I came away in awe with a new sense of humility.

The first time in history, anywhere on Earth, where people were guaranteed a trial by a jury of peers came at Runnymede (England) with the agreement of Magna Carta between several English Barons and King John of England on June 15, 1215. There are 63 stipulations contained in and agreed to in Magna Carta. Stipulation #39: "No freeman shall be taken or imprisoned or disseised or exiled or in any way destroyed, nor will we go upon him nor send upon him, *except by the lawful judgment of his peers* or by the law of the land."

By digging a little deeper I discovered events that have transpired through history and time to the present day. Why, exactly, did King John agree to Magna Carta and what was it? It all started around 1100 A.D. with King John's father—King Henry I.

Background:
There has always been contention on the flow of English history because Latin was the primary written language and historical documents have left much to be argued. Henry I of England, nicknamed Beauclerc (for his scholarly interests) and Lion of Justice (for refinements which he brought about in the administrative and legislative machinery of the time) was the fourth and youngest son of William the Conqueror. The name Beauclerc was given because Henry was well educated, being able to read and write Latin, and possessed a knowledge of English law and natural history. He had received 5000 pounds of silver from his father, but no land holdings. He used this to purchase a district in Contentin in Normandy for 3000 pounds from his brother, Robert of Normandy. The latter had been given the Duchy (a domain controlled by a Duke or Dutchess) of Normandy by his father, William the Conqueror, but had fallen into pecuniary difficulty (money problems). Various political intrigues occurred in France, which led to the imprisonment of Henry for two years by his other brother William Rufus, who had taken the throne of England upon the death of their brother, Richard. William Rufus assumed the name William II of England. Robert of Normandy left for the Crusade in 1096. Henry pledged an oath of fealty (loyalty) to Rufus who came to hold Normandy in the absence of Robert. William II of England died while hunting on August 2, 1100 (an arrow killed him); Henry was present on this hunting trip. This was similar to the way the eldest son of William I, Richard, had died in 1081. The death of William II and the power vacuum from Robert's absence (fighting in the Crusades) allowed Henry to claim the English Crown in 1100.

Henry was immediately faced with three political problems: (1) His barons and earls did not accept him. (2) There was antagonism from the

Catholic Church, especially over issues with Anselm of Canterbury (the bishop). (3) The native Anglo-Saxon population was not conducive to the new king.

Henry made concessions to the Church by reconciling with Anselm. He accepted as his wife Edith, who was of mixed Anglo-Scots heritage and the daughter of Malcolm III, King of the Scots. This garnered great favor with the Anglo-Saxon population which viewed Edith as one of their own. The choice displeased the barons and earls. Edith changed her name to the Norman name Mathilda. In order to ameliorate them, Henry entered into an agreement with the barons and earls. The Charter of Liberties was that agreement where King Henry agreed to be bound by the rule of law. That never happened, but the seed had been planted.

King Henry I had many children, most illegitimate, but four direct heirs to the English throne: Henry, Richard, Arthur and John. On King Henry I's death, his son Henry took the throne as King Henry II (ruling from 1154-1189) and was the first ruler to be called "King of England." On Henry's death in July 1189, the English throne went to Richard, also known as "Richard The Lionheart" because of his military prowess and fearlessness in battle. King Richard ruled England from 1189-1199 with an interesting anecdotal story.

Of King Henry I four heirs to the throne, John was the worst of the lot, a man not to be trusted, evil and of nasty disposition. Realizing this, King Richard had his brother John banished from England and sent him to exile in Ireland while he went off to fight the Crusades. During this time John plotted and had his brother, Arthur (the next heir to the throne), murdered. Richard, meanwhile, was captured on his return from the Crusades and held captive for five years. When he returned to England, his life lasted only a short while and John claimed the throne in 1199 on Richard's death.

John ruled with an iron hand and went off with his army to capture France, where he was soundly defeated. On his return to England, King John was broke and did something that changed the course of history. He issued scuttage against many of the barons and earls of England. Scuttage was a tax to be paid in lieu of military service. King John directly taxed the barons of England who would not serve or back him in battle and a civil war would have started, saved only by John's agreement to Magna Carta. John's thought was that by agreement to Magna Carta he was simply "buying time" and its provisions were meaningless to him. During his early reign, King John had alienated the Catholic Church to the point where he was excommunicated. John made a new allegiance with the Pope by making concessions dealing with the Bishop of Canterbury, and asked the Pope for a favor. When John had Magna Carta voided by the Pope, a political error that backfired, civil war broke out in England and ended on John's death in September 1216 where his only son, also named Henry, became England's youngest king at the age of 9 years. King Henry III (the boy king) ruled England for 56 years until his death and spent a great deal of that time fighting the barons over Magna Carta. That political fight finally ended with the establishment of the English Parliament in 1264.

Magna Carta, also called Magna Carta Libertatum (the Great Charter of Freedoms), is an English legal charter, written in Latin and is known by its Latin name. The usual English translation of Magna Carta is Great Charter. It required King John of England to proclaim certain rights pertaining to freemen, respect certain legal procedures, and accept that his will could be bound by the law. It explicitly protected certain rights of the King's subjects, whether free or fettered and implicitly supported what became the writ of habeas corpus, allowing appeal against unlawful imprisonment. The concept of "due process" had been born.

Magna Carta was arguably the most significant early influence on the extensive historical process that led to the rule of constitutional law today in the English speaking world. Magna Carta influenced the development of common law and many constitutional documents, including the United States Constitution. Many clauses were renewed throughout the Middle Ages, and continued to be renewed as late as the 18th century. By the second half of the 19th century, however, most clauses in their original form had been repealed or redrafted by English law.

In practice, Magna Carta in the medieval period mostly did not limit the power of Kings; but by the time of the English Civil War it had become an important symbol for those who wished to show that their King was bound by the rule of law. It was the first document of freedom ever recorded anywhere in the world and is the foundation on which our Constitution was drafted.

Thomas Jefferson used Magna Carta as the cornerstone to the Declaration of Independence. Abraham Lincoln, used Magna Carta and the Declaration of Independence as cornerstones when drafting the Gettysburg Address and the Emancipation Proclamation.

Let me carry these points just a bit further. The Pledge of Allegiance is an oath of loyalty to our national flag and the Republic of the United States of America. It was drafted by Francis Bellamy 1892. What most people don't know is that the Pledge was written to celebrate the 400th anniversary of the landing of Christopher Columbus. The Pledge has been modified four times since then, with the most recent change adding the words "under God" in 1954. Those two words have caused a great deal of furor in our country by those who believe there is no God. Again, what most people don't know is that those two words came from Lincoln's Gettysburg Address.

Chapter 36: Heroes

I have always been fascinated through historical education and my appetite for it became voracious as I learned more and more. There are so many instances in our country where things could have been different if it were not for the many "heroes" that stood their ground and were unrelenting in their quest for justice and freedom, concepts that are unfortunately lost on the youth of today.

Of my personal heroes, I will mention only three of them here for what they unselfishly did for freedom: John Adams, George Mason and Richard Henry Lee. Christopher has heard me speak of them many times, especially John Adams as a member of the Committee of Five, later on that though. Most everyone knows Adams was our 2nd president and the only Puritan at that. George Mason was the greatest American never to be president and yet few people know who he was or what he did. Richard Henry Lee's voice at the 2nd Continental Congress broadcast to the world of the colonies break from England.

I won't mention much about John Adams because there is a mini-series that does him a great justice. Suffice it to say that without John Adams and his driving desire for freedom from England, there probably would not have been adoption of the Declaration of Independence in July 1776.

George Mason was an oak. As a wealthy land owner from Virginia, the largest, wealthiest and most influential colony in the Americas, George Mason was the cornerstone for our country. He was a scholarly giant, as well as was a contemporary of Washington and Jefferson and we can thank him for the Bill of Rights. Mason wrote the constitution for the state of Virginia and the Virginia Declaration of Rights, "the" gospel for civil rights that was adopted in one form or another by most of the colonies as their constitutions were written. If any man deserves to have his name mentioned in the same sentence as George Washington, Thomas Jefferson, James Madison, Benjamin Franklin, Thomas Paine, or any of the other Founding Fathers, it would be George Mason. Let me elaborate a bit.

Jefferson knew him personally. So did Washington, Madison, Paine, Henry, the Adamses, and the others at the 2nd Continental Congress. Mason was a Virginian. He was 18 years older than Jefferson and had a profound influence on him. Jefferson never made a secret of the fact that he revered him. He called Mason the wisest man of his generation. Even Madison, who is generally credited with framing the Bill of Rights, and who became the fourth President, considered Mason one of the most profound and penetrating thinkers of his time. And he was right. Washington himself called upon him many times. In fact, many of the Founding Fathers, whose names nowadays roll off the tongues of school children, knew who he was, were influenced by him, and sought his advice.

Mason's fellow Virginians, and this included the lawyers, deferred to him with the acknowledgment that no one else in the colony knew the colonial laws as well as he. It was also a tacit acknowledgment of his capabilities and honesty. In a six week period, during May and June of 1776, he wrote the state's constitution and its bill of rights, called the Virginia Declaration of Rights.

The Declaration of Rights was adopted in June, three weeks before the Declaration of Independence was signed at the Continental Congress. In it Mason held that 'All men are by nature born equally free and independent' and 'that all power was originally lodged in, and consequently derived from, the people. If those words sound familiar, it's because Jefferson paraphrased them in the preamble to the Declaration of Independence.

The others at the Continental Congress knew where the words came from. Mason's Declaration had been copied and sent to the other colonies. Up and down the Atlantic seaboard it was read aloud in public places, printed in newspapers, considered, debated, and admired. There wasn't a man at the Congress who hadn't seen the Declaration or knew who its author was. And one after another, first Pennsylvania, then Maryland, then

Delaware, then North Carolina and others took most or all of the Virginia Declaration of Rights and either made them amendments to their own constitutions or incorporated them directly into their constitutions.

Jefferson had endorsed the concept of the Bill of Rights, but he wasn't the originator. Madison had steered it through the Congress, but the ideas weren't his either. As a matter of fact, the irony is that even though Madison honchoed the legislation through the Congress, he originally opposed including a bill of rights in the Constitution. George Mason, as patriotic a man who ever lived, did not support ratification of the Constitution because it contained no human rights, none, zero, zip.

As a refresher, I'll explain that the United States Constitution, in its original form, contained just seven Articles and no mention of individual rights can be found as set out below.

Article 1: Defines and discusses the legislative branch (Congress)
Article 2: Defines and discusses the executive branch (President)
Article 3: Defines and discusses the judicial branch (Supreme Court)
Article 4: Defines and discusses state powers
Article 5: Defines and discusses how the Constitution can be amended
Article 6: Establishes the Constitution as the supreme law of the land
Article 7: Defines how the Constitution is ratified (9 of 13 colonies)

All of this, of course, you learned in school (if you paid attention). What is glaringly missing in the original Constitution is any mention of civil rights. Enter George Mason. Speaking out in opposition to constitutional ratification on the grounds that civil rights were not included, Mason was joined by the likes of Patrick Henry ("Give me liberty or give me death") and Thomas Paine (Common Sense). Their voices prompted Alexander Hamilton, James Madison and John Jay to publish what later became known as the Federalist Papers that advocated ratification of the U.S. Constitution. Mason stood fast in his beliefs and opposition to ratification, but was not successful. He was successful, however, in keeping Virginia, the wealthiest and most influential colony, from ratifying the Constitution until 9 other colonies had done so. Even in the face of defeat, Mason never gave up. He was the voice of descent and finally convinced Madison he was right. Madison, who initially opposed a declaration of rights, offered more than 20 amendments to the Constitution to Congress. Of those offered, 12 went forward to the states for ratification and 10 were ratified. Those 10 amendments are known as The Bill of Rights. Without George Mason, it wouldn't exist, and our form of government in all likelihood, would have failed.

Richard Henry Lee of Virginia authored The Lee Resolution, also known as the resolution of independence, during a session of the 2nd Continental Congress on June 7, 1776 and offered the resolution that changed history. His resolution says:

"Resolved, that these United Colonies are, and of right ought to be, free and independent States, that they are absolved from all allegiance to the British Crown, and that all political connection between them and the State of Great Britain is, and ought to be, totally dissolved."

His statement caused a great deal of furor at the convention that was quieted only when John Hancock, President of the 2nd Continental Congress, called for a cooling off period of three weeks. On June 11, 1776, Hancock appointed the Committee of Five to draft a document explaining to the world the reasons for independence from England. The committee consisted of John Adams of Massachusetts, Benjamin Franklin of Pennsylvania, Robert Livingston of New York, and Roger Sherman of Connecticut. The fifth member would have been Richard Henry Lee, but he was called home due to a family illness. His replacement on the committee was Thomas Jefferson of Virginia.

A note about Robert Livingston: he was Chancellor (governor) of New York and was the man who gave George Washington the oath of office as the first President of the United States. The Washington Inauguration took place on April 30, 1790, in New York City, the first United States capital and the site of the first congress.

At the behest of the committee, Jefferson, alone, drafted the Declaration of Independence and when completed, sent copies to Adams and Franklin for review and revision. The Lee Resolution, in its entirety, was adopted on July 2, 1776. Two passages in the Committee of Five's draft of the Declaration of Independence were rejected by the Congress. One was an intemperate reference to the English people and the other was a scathing denunciation of the slave trade. The Declaration of Independence was otherwise adopted without major change two days later when the Congress reached agreement during the late morning of July 4th, following intensive review sessions conducted during the afternoons of July 2nd and July 3rd.

Few people, save for historical scholars, are aware of the impact of Richard Henry Lee. His importance was given a glint of recognition when the 20th Amendment of the Constitution was ratified on January 23, 1933. With the adoption of the 20th Amendment, the newly elected President of the United States is inaugurated on the 20th day of January following his election, the birth date of Richard Henry Lee. The Lee Resolution is quoted verbatim in the final paragraph of the Declaration of Independence.

Of course, I could go on and on and on. The early history of our country fascinates me no end and it's a major miracle it all worked out. That miracle would not have happened though without the tireless effort put forth at the 2nd Continental Congress by John Adams. So I've come full circle honoring a few of my personal heroes. My wish is that the two of you will look inward and not outward and find your heroes.

Everyone should have heroes in his or her life, someone who is personally admired and respected, or a person who has touched them deeply. These are three of mine, along with Leo Buscaglia and Russell Herman Conwell.

Your dad has taken some unpopular stances in life and in his profession with the Superior Court, but all of them, without fail, were because of what he believed to be the right thing to do. Not the popular thing, but the right thing, and I have the emotional scars to prove it. I have no regrets.

Chapter 37: A Tearful, Painful Split

Fractured relationships are heartbreaking and this one would be no exception. I always loved being married; I just wasn't very good at it. This is about as good a place to start using song lyrics to openly express my emotions. Our move to Palos Verdes came at a bad time in the real estate market (always seemed that way for me). We sold the Vallecito home for what we owed on it after I had sunk a small fortune into remodeling the place. Mary Anne found a house in Palos Verdes that she persisted on having. The $100,000 for the down payment came from Legaltech, my computer business. It was thriving and so I gave her the money. We moved to 3212 Seaclaire Drive and the first thing we did was drop $5K to have the inside painted and $15K for new, plush green carpeting. The expenses were unbelievable and went on and on and on, just like movie The Money Pit. When I mentioned this to Mary Anne all she said (again) was, "Sell more networks." Between my job with the Superior Court and my computer business I was making in excess of $25,000 a month which may not be a great deal to a lot of people, but it was a fortune to me. Mary Anne was an attorney, but her income did not play in our family. I was near the breaking point and tried to reason with her; she was not interested. She liked the arrangement just as it was. I still cared for her and I absolutely loved my daughter, but I had hit the wall. I had done everything I knew how, but just couldn't find a way to make it work. Everything I did was just stupid wrong.

> I don't know what else I can say to you,
> I'm doing everything I know to do,
> And I can't give you anything more,
> When I'm giving my best . . .
>
> . . . Ricky Van Shelton

Although my emotional state was like scrambled eggs, Alicia was a bundle of happiness and her presence eased my troubled mind. She was my sunshine when there was none. I had said those very words in 1980 when my step-sister, Vanessa, unexpectedly left this world and now my daughter had stepped into that role without realizing it. Well, how could she know? She was just a baby! The feelings I held for her were exactly the same as I had when Chris was born. Silently I shed tears for the uncertain future I knew was coming. (Trouble In Paradise—The Crests)

Just as it happened in 1979 when Penny and I split, it was clear to me that I had misjudged my relationship with Mary Anne. Where Penny had tried to be a team player, Mary Anne did not. My pleas fell on deft ears that were quick to change the subject or reject it out of hand. Mary Anne just would not share, or perhaps while growing up she had never learned how. My marriage to her failed simply because we were not a team and for no other reason. Did I love her? Yes, of course, but it had become a faded love. Near the end of our relationship Mary Anne tried to get a message to me by playing a CD she bought that contained a song that she wanted me to hear. The lyrics to such a beautiful song were transmitted far too late to save us, and every time I hear it I am reminded of my failures.

> Baby tell me where'd you ever learn to fight without sayin'
> a word?
> And waltz back into my life like it's all gonna be alright.
> Don't you know how much it hurts?
>
> . . . Faith Hill

In all honestly, it mattered to me, too. It had mattered for a very long time. Of course I loved Mary Anne. My heart, though, could not take the continual rejection of not sharing. If only she . . . Never mind. I tearfully, too, left Mary Anne a message; I doubt she understood. If she did, she never showed any emotion.

> It's just not working, we've both known for sometime.
> That old fire's been out for so long, we've just stopped trying.
> The only time we're touching, is when we're passing in the hall.

And yesterday's "I love you's" don't really matter at all.

         . . . Billy Joe Royal

So I left. It was the first and only time in my life that I truly gave up on anything. I stayed nearby to be close to Alicia, but Mary Anne did her best to keep Alicia out of my life. I took Buscaglia's advice and wouldn't look back.

> "You have your paint and brushes. You paint paradise. If you
> want, you can paint Heaven or you can paint Hell, but if
> you do paint Hell, don't blame me, don't blame society and
> don't blame God. Blame yourself. If you don't like the stage
> you're on, get new colors and repaint it, surround yourself
> with new actors and start all over again . . ."
>
>   . . . Leo Buscaglia

That's exactly what I did. I put the blame squarely where it belonged and started on a long and difficult emotional journey to build a new life.

As emotionally difficult as it was, I was finding peace, but a war was brewing. Mary Anne wanted a fight. She hired a vicious family law attorney and she wanted Alicia, she wanted my retirement, she wanted spousal support (even though she was a working attorney), and she wanted to hurt. She got nearly everything she wanted and I let her have it. I worked out the best arrangements I could. In our discussions with our respective attorneys, Mary Anne wanted money, a great deal of it, from Legaltech. I owned all of the stock (Legaltech was a California Corporation) and her attorney wanted a piece of the action. Well, I'm not the brightest guy in the world, but I saw through this immediately. I told her attorney that Mary Anne was welcome to all of the Legaltech stock. The corporation was hers. She could have it. Mary Anne said, "If you don't run Legaltech, it won't make any money." Truer words were never spoken. I closed down my corporation on the spot and walked away from it. Game over. Now you may think the attorneys were in charge of our court proceedings, but they were fighting between themselves. Finally, I convinced Mary Anne to come to an agreement (I offered her $40,000 to walk away). She said she would for $50,000 (still selfish and greedy). I agreed, but raw emotions raged on for some time. She may have come out much better than I money wise, but I came out with something I dearly needed, freedom and peace of mind. I had let it go. After all, I thought, it's just chips. I was a money making machine and knew I could rebuild it all if I wanted, but the desire to do so was gone.

Splitting up with someone you have spent many years with is both horribly distressful and gut-wrenching. Time heals all wounds, or so they say. After a while, my hurt feelings started to subside and I played the following song over and over and over. One more hurt, one more broken relationship, and no one to blame but myself.

> Up along the hallway, down along the stairs,
> I can see the pictures, we made down through the years,
> And it makes me blue darling, thinking of the past,
> And I'm truly sorry, I couldn't make it last.

A hundred years from now, no one will have any memory of these events or the feelings that spilled across the lives of two people who should have made it, but didn't. Sometimes I reflect back on everything that happened and I am amazed by the whole fiasco. When my relationship started with Mary Anne, I owned a beautiful townhouse in Palos Verdes. When it was over, I had nothing. And quite remarkably, I also had no regrets.

What I did have was a beautiful daughter and I looked hopefully to the future, as I always have. Leo Buscaglia had a monumental impact on how I dealt with adversity. I would need that resolve as once again another tearful moment was about to descend on me. Thanks to Dr. Buscaglia, I had learned how to "let go." If I had had the opportunity to say any last works to Mary Anne (I didn't), they would be from a Clint Black song. I was sad, but grateful in many ways.

> I guess I always knew I couldn't hold you,
> But I'd never be the one to set you free.
> Just like some old nursery rhyme your mama told you,
> You still believe in some old meant-to-be . . .
> . . . Clint Black

My nine year marriage to Mary Anne was longer than some had predicted, and yet I came away from it a much stronger individual. She taught me ways to release tension and assisted me in difficult situations in court management. From 1989-1993 I made well over 1.5 million dollars in a small computer business and it was all gone. The money was still there to be made if I wanted it, but I no longer had the desire. Money just didn't matter. My worst loss was the time I could not reclaim and life was for living, not remembering.

As I wrote this part of my story, I actually put forth a sincere effort to show both sides, mine and BSA's. However, I am wise enough to know there are three sides to this story: my side, her side, and the truth. By telling as much as I could in the third person, I strived to relieve some of the emotional moments, but that task is ever so difficult. Oh, what do I mean by BSA? Simple: Blood Sucking Attorney, my pet name for Mary Anne. I guess I didn't succeed after all. Oh, well. After all these years and all the experiences and all the learning, Steven was still an idiot.

Chapter 38: Demoted (sort of)

While the turmoil between Mary Anne and I was raging, I was blind-sided at Jury operations. Because of court unification, we had a new executive officer who was not particularly fond of superior court managers, me in particular. What really bothered Ed Kritzman was the fact that I had a very close and unique relationship with the judiciary; I had many close friends on the bench all across Los Angeles County. Instead of using that to his advantage, he chose to eliminate it.

Well, there had been an earthquake in Los Angeles on January 17, 1994, that had devastated the courthouse in San Fernando. It would be 5 years before it would reopen. In the meantime, I was now the administrator in the jury division. Because jury operations were the main focus of Judge Klausner's plan, I set my goals to restructure and improve the system as best I could. The Jury Call Center was my biggest contribution to his plan and I am very proud of that achievement.

I had been reassigned from Torrance to downtown, but still had close contacts in the South Bay. I persuaded the South Bay Municipal Court's facilities manager, Joe Unger, to follow me downtown and he did. Joe was given a special assignment as I directed him to travel to each jury assembly room across the county and provide me with a complete and comprehensive inventory of each facility along with his recommendations on how to improve the facilities. His recommendations were sound and straight to the point.

One morning over coffee, Joe told me the facilities in the Long Beach Courthouse were deplorable. He said the jury staff had to give the jury orientation at least twice a day, sometimes more. The jury room

156

had space, but not nearly enough chairs. I mentioned this fact to Jim Dempsey, Assistant Executive Officer, and told him I had a way to resolve the situation. He told me to go for it, and I contacted the Central District facilities manager downtown and arranged for a truck to move all of the furniture from the San Fernando Courthouse (wasn't being used anyway) to the Long Beach Courthouse. Problem solved. It was a disaster. Not for the court, but for me. Because I didn't tell Ed Kritzman about the move, he popped his cork when he found out and called me on the carpet for it.

I was summoned to his office and he and I had a heated discussion. At the end he raised his voice and said, "Before I do you . . ." I stopped him cold. To everyone I have ever mentored or taught, I have ALWAYS stressed that there is no excuse to be rude to anyone, ever. Well, if you push this old dog into a corner, he's gonna bite. So I made myself an exception! Ed Kritzman was the Executive Officer and a complete jerk so I stood up in front of him and said, "Take your best shot, you little twerp. Others have tried." He was a little guy with a Napoleon syndrome, probably 5'6" or so and I towered over him. He was stunned and totally speechless, and then I walked out.

The next day, a friend of mine named John Sleeter, was put in charge of jury operations. John was a brilliant guy, but completely lost when dealing with people. As for me, I was reassigned to the Central Civil Courthouse doing special projects, basically doing nothing for the next three years. I was in limbo or in the twilight zone as I called it. Was I depressed or down on myself for being put on skid row? Not in the least as I had learned to roll with the flow. I became an expert on reading the newspapers.

Within the next year, Ed Kritzman would "retire" from the courts, pushed out is more like it. There would be a new executive officer in our courts by the name of John Clarke from New Jersey. On my first sight of him, I was a little baffled after hearing all the plaudits from everyone. He was getting out of an old, beat-up white Nissan Altima and wearing a green polyester suit. Where did they get him, I wondered? He came with a great deal of support from the AOC (Administrative Office of the Courts) and the Judiciary in New Jersey. He was loud, obnoxious and not pleasant to most. I was still in limbo, buried doing special projects, but I didn't resent it. I was pretty good at getting just about anything done and I excelled at statistical analysis. After all, I was an economics major and statistics were right up my alley. When my turn came to be interviewed by Mr. Clarke, our discussions turned on his preconceived impression of me from the previous executive officer. His manner of subjecting managers to unrelenting pressure didn't work on me. I was my own person and not intimidated by anyone, least of all him and I told him so. "You're judging me from what you've heard from Ed Kritzman and that doesn't speak well of you, Mr. Clarke," I told him and I continued when given the opportunity to speak, " . . . and you're surrounding yourself here with mediocre people who are not a threat to you, mostly women, some of whom have risen on their backs. Everyone you meet greets you pleasantly with a smile, but that is not how they talk about you." He took it all in silently.

When he asked me what I would like to do, I mentioned a desire to manage the technology area of the court. "That's not in the cards," he said bluntly. After a two-hour talk with him, I had a fairly good idea of what he would be like. He, on the other hand, had no idea of my abilities. A few months later I would make him look like a hero.

Chapter 39: Automation Committee

Technology was abounding in the judicial system and on-line legal research was a hot commodity. One afternoon in passing, Mr. Clarke stopped me on the steps of the courthouse and asked me to see his secretary, Michelle, and set an appointment to meet with him. When we met later in the week he mentioned a discussion he had recently with Judge Judith Ashman regarding Lexis-Nexis, easily the most expensive and thorough on-line legal research software application on the market. Since the Los Angeles Superior Court had more than 650 judges, the court wanted a contract if the negotiations went well. Judge Ashman was chair of the Court Automation Committee, and she was a friend of mine. She told Mr. Clarke that she wanted one of the court administrators to join the committee and sit-in on the negotiations. She said the judges were at a disadvantage discussing technology and they needed support. She told him that whomever he selected it would be his choice, but that person had to be both technologically capable and understand the judge's perspective on computers. Well, he asked her opinion. "Steve Forrest," she said. "You have no one else close to him."

Mr. Clarke told me I would be sitting in on the next meeting with Lexis-Nexis management at Judge Ashman's request. Okay. I was out of limbo and at the first meeting, I saved the court $500,000 and opened the gates to a legal research bonanza. To me it wasn't a big deal, just common sense.

Judy Ashman called me and gave me the news before Mr. Clarke did, but I didn't say a word about it to anyone. The meeting was scheduled for 2:00 p.m. on Friday and Judge Ashman and I had a nice talk at lunch that day. She said she was a little apprehensive with Lexis and didn't want to be taken advantage of in any way. "Won't be an issue, I assured her." I had met Judge Ashman years before when I was "floating" around the county gaining experience in different types of litigation and worked in her criminal trial court for a couple weeks when her clerk was on vacation. One afternoon while we were chatting, she mentioned she had an 8-year old son (Tommy) who loved kid movies and would watch them over and over. She also knew I was the computer guy as the judges referred to me and asked if I could get her a good one. Of course I could and did. When I drove to her home in Westwood, near UCLA, and installed her computer, she introduced me to her husband who was a sports attorney/agent. His biggest client to that point in time was Vida Blue who pitched for the Oakland Athletics. He enjoyed telling how free-agency in sports would make millions for the athletes, and with a wink said "and their agents."

The Lexis-Nexis meeting started promptly at 2:00 p.m. with six members of Lexis management in attendance. Judge Ashman, John Clarke, Judy Call (upper management) were there representing the court. Oh, and me, too. During the discussions, which had been going on for more than a year, the Lexis staff laid out their newest proposal where the judges would need to purchase and install high-speed modems for their computers in chambers in addition to the Lexis-Nexis software to access the legal research database on-line. Training would also be needed and that would cost an additional sum to be determined later. The numbers that were flying all around were staggering: $150K for the software, $130K for modems, $100K for training, and other incidentals. As I listened, it was easy to understand the committee's position, they wanted the contract, yet were uncertain on how to proceed. When the opportunity presented itself, and it did, I said, "May I interrupt, please. I have a few questions." I was given the floor and smiled at Judge Ashman as I started.

"As I understand the situation at present, Lexis expects the court to buy the judges high-speed modems to access the Lexis database on-line; but not just the judges will need access. We also have a slew of research attorneys who will need access, as well as all the commissioners in the court." Everyone was now watching with a great deal of interest. "Additionally," I continued, "the modems will have to be continually upgraded as dial-up speed increases. That's a lot of wasted money when a simple solution is available that will cost far less. May I make a suggestion? The Lexis offices are right down the street, about 6 blocks from here. Is that a correct statement? (Approval nodded) And I assume Lexis can broadcast from their offices with a T-1 line. Is that also a correct assumption? (Again, positive nod from Lexis, the court staff sat in silence.) With that in mind, why can't Lexis install a gateway here at the court?" "Go on," the Lexis staff said.

"I'll put this in perspective so the committee has a complete picture (I didn't say understanding as that would have been offensive). The court already has a wide-area network so the judges can send e-mails to each other around the county. If Lexis puts in a gateway to our network downtown, every judge, commissioner and research attorney in the court who needs access to Lexis can do so without a modem! They would be able to access it directly from the court's network at an incredibly faster speed. No outlay for modems which would require continual upgrades, and no monthly outlay for an ISP for each judge to access the Internet, and no outlay for software. The Lexis software just needs to be installed here and nowhere else."

The Lexis staff member in charge spoke up and said, "Where have you been for the past year? We have been discussing this contract for 15 months and baby-stepping it along the way. Everything you just said is doable and would make this a slam-dunk, a win-win for everyone. Anything else to add?"

"Yes, if I may," and I continued, "If this were to go forward as I mentioned, a lot of time and effort would be saved because the software would not have to be purchased and installed on every judge's computer. Having said that, a licensing agreement could be arranged that "should" including free training from Lexis."

"We can do that," was the Lexis response, "and I'm sure we can negotiate an agreeable license agreement. You don't have any more ideas, do you?"

"Just one," I continued, "Lexis will install their gateway computer here at no charge to the court, I assume. The court will have to lease a T-1 line from the phone company, but that shouldn't be an issue." Judge Ashman was beaming and Mr. Clarke looked at me, but remained silent. After all, I was a network guy and understood it all perfectly.

The next week I was again summoned to Mr. Clarke's office. I was informed that the Court Automation Committee was going forward with my suggestions and if an agreement was reached, Lexis-Nexis training would be conducted at each court location. "You're in charge of the judge's training, Steve," Mr. Clarke informed me. Judge Ashman had insisted on it. For now, I was out of the dog-house and things were starting to look up (good thing your dad wasn't shy).

The assignment given to me was enjoyable, interesting, and gave me an opportunity to better understand the judge's position on automation. Some of my conversations were strikingly off the cuff.

I fondly remember chatting with Judge Robert Fratianne one afternoon about his daughter, Linda, who had placed 2nd at the 1980 Olympics in Lake Placid, New York. Judge Fratianne spoke of her coach, Frank Carroll, and how Linda was now working with him. She won the Olympics, but "the judges screwed her" was his favorite line.

Once again I was enjoying myself on the job, but that was coming to an end as a new assignment was about to be leveled on me, one that would be more challenging than any before.

Chapter 40: Doug McKee

There must have been a divorce disease descending on my part of the globe as my best friend, Doug McKee, was also going through a contentious divorce from his wife of 25 years. After splitting with Sheila, he had moved into a marvelous townhouse complex in Rolling Hills Estates overlooking the ocean. Mike Torres and I helped him move and remodel. We spent several evenings and weekends helping Doug fix-up his new abode. We R&R'd (removed and replaced) all the sinks, toilets, and cabinets. We also laid new tile flooring and painted the place. For all of our efforts, the place was dazzling. It was bright, cheerful and carried an inviting feel to it. His two sons, Grant and Drake, chose to live with him and not with their mother. At first glance, it appeared Doug was doing just fine. Doug, however, was not okay.

One day while spending my lunch hour with friends in the confines of the conference room (Room 116) downtown, I received a telephone call from the District Attorney's Office that rocked my world. I was informed that Doug McKee, my best friend and confidant, had committed suicide that very morning. The Sheriff had found Doug's corvette along Palos Verdes Drive North, abandoned near the cliffs. They knew immediately that it was Doug's car from the license plate that read DAMSCJ (Douglas A. McKee, Superior Court Judge). Doug was a proud man, proud of his place in life, proud of his position with the court, proud of his corvette, proud of his friends, but Doug could not cope with losing his family. The news hit like a ton of bricks and I was coming apart fast. Immediately I announced to those present that I was leaving. As I was heading to the door, I heard someone call, "Steve." I stopped and turned to be greeted by Carol Cacheiro, one of the managers in the Central District. Carol and I had been friends as well as co-workers, and we served on a committee together. She had always been pleasant, courteous and professional on the job. Above all else, she possessed one the most cherished attributes a person can have: honesty. When she stopped me that morning, she hugged me, and looked into the eyes of a man whose spirit had just been crushed. Pain was written all over my face she would later tell me. Her gentle manner of reassurance softly touched me. I didn't know it then, but I had found Dr. Buscaglia's dream person, someone who possessed beauty and joy and spirituality and those attributes radiated from her.

I left the courthouse and made a bee-line to the McKee residence in Rolling Hills Estates. His ex-wife, the malcontented Sheila McKee, was present as were his two sons, Grant and Drake. I recognized several others in attendance (lawyers, DAs, PDs, and Judge Frank Baffa). In all of the chaos and confusion, no one had taken the lead regarding Doug's funeral arrangements. I wasn't part of Doug's family, but I was his best friend. Without hesitation or reservation, I spoke to Grant and Drake alone; I asked if anything had been done. Nothing yet was the response and then Grant asked me if I would help them with the arrangements. He told me they trusted me and wanted their dad cremated so they could spread his ashes in Yosemite. I made all of the arrangements and delivered Doug's eulogy at Green Hills. Doug had worked diligently to establish and maintain a close, personal relationship with law enforcement. He had many friends on the Torrance Police Department, the Sheriff's Department, the California Highway Patrol and the LAPD. Those friends and many, many others packed the chapel at Green Hills. I still recall the opening words of praise I gave them as the ceremony commenced:

"Welcome everyone. Thank you for your presence. Grant and Drake McKee are very appreciative of all the members of law enforcement who have taken time out of their lives to honor a fallen friend. You are each an honored guest . . ."

I don't really remember much after that except for the one song I had played over the chapel's sound system for his sons: The Wind Beneath My Wings (Gary Morris). There wasn't a dry eye in the place and when the ceremony concluded, Gary Klausner came up to me and said, "I'm sorry, Steve," and shook my hand. I could not respond. It was Doug's funeral, but I shared it with him and I was an emotional mess. Doug had needed help and I didn't see it. I was so close to him and yet I was absolutely blind. I was so ego-involved in my own troubles that I just wasn't looking. Drake and Grant were so relieved and grateful for my assistance, they gave me Doug's Corvette.

Out of that experience walked a man with new convictions and a new prospective on life. My personality was evolving from a strongly dominant person to one who would look more, see more, and feel more. No longer would the world revolve around me (foolish thought, I know, it never really did) and I had awakened the humility that was ever present in me, yet so often ignored. I assured myself that at every opportunity I would be the one who would create impetus for others, and wherever I could help, I would. My transition had started, but the process would take a very long time; I'm not certain it will ever be completed.

I don't recall exactly when the next changing event in my life took place, because it was innocuous and unplanned. While speaking to my good friend, Jim Piper, he mentioned that he and his wife, Ann, were going to a dinner party at Carol Cacheiro's home in Diamond Bar. Jim and Carol had worked together in the Norwalk court. All I knew about Diamond Bar was that Alta Sport was there (the place I bought most of my ski gear) and Dave Cummins, once my roommate, had lived there. So out to Diamond Bar I went. I had to find Sugar Pine Place and make a turn up the hill. Simple enough . . .

Life isn't about how you survived the storm . . . it's about how you danced in the rain!

Chapter 41: Long Beach

At some point in your life, you will be exposed to opportunities that seem to come out of the blue and sometimes they won't look like opportunities at all. Having been down dark and uncertain trails before, I'd come to expect the unexpected, but because of Leo Buscaglia, always with awe and mostly with a wry grin. Life didn't present me with problems, just challenges and choices. Although I could have made better choices, I relished challenges. Nothing ventured, nothing gained. Not always successful, I was the "go for it" guy. Failure was never because of a lack of effort; it was probably due more to a lack of adequate planning. There is always a successful path to any challenge.

So after a couple months of spearheading the judge's Lexis-Nexis training, I was again called to Mr. Clarke's office where he informed me there was a crisis in the Long Beach Court that needed attention. Seems the Superior Court Administrator, Tim Adams, had difficulty interfacing with the Long Beach Municipal Court Administrator. He said he wanted to give me an opportunity to move back into operations by replacing Adams. As I listened to his story, suspicion crept into my thoughts. The story he related to me was unpleasantly strange.

"You want me to be your 'hit man' in Long Beach, don't you?" I asked. He looked at me for the longest time before he said, "Mr. Adams is a little weak in dealing with the municipal court." I told him, "Tim Adams isn't weak, he's a wimp. He's smart and a really nice guy, but a wimp none the less. Straight and to the point, Mr. Clarke. I've done this job before, but before I go head long into it, I want your assurance that you're backing me." He told me the orders to put me in Long Beach came from the top,

166

the presiding judge. Whether or not that was true didn't really matter. This was an unforseen opportunity.

Without hesitation, he informed me that he still was not sure about me and this assignment would be a deal maker, one way or the other. Well, I wasn't so sure about him either and I told him so. Mr. Clarke and I were always straightforwardly blunt with one another and I don't believe he cared for my way of expressing myself to him. Then I asked him an unanswered question when I said, "Why do you surround yourself with mediocre people?" The first time I had laid eyes on John Clarke, he was getting out of a dingy white Altima and wearing a green polyester suit. He reminded me of Homer Simpson.

Here's another lesson for you two. There will be times in your career when you will be asked or required to do unpleasant tasks, sometimes distasteful tasks, but if you don't do them, the opportunity will go to someone else. And that's exactly what they are—opportunities. Obviously, this was another unpleasant opportunity. Because I am goal oriented, my feeling and belief is that any assignment given to me, no matter how unpleasant, will be accomplished and I will do whatever is necessary as long as it doesn't have any moral or legal complications. During each assignment I've received, my loyalty on the job always went to the Superior Court and I did my absolute best to improve every area where I was assigned, but more importantly, I received a great deal of pride in helping others move along their career path.

The next week I was in the South District (Long Beach) where I knew few of the employees and even fewer judges. Superficially, this appeared to be the most challenging assignment of my career as the Long Beach Municipal Court Administrator, Sharon Gonterman, had been entrenched there for many years and enjoyed a terrific relationship with the judiciary, both in the municipal court and the superior court. However, she had two things going against her: she was over-confident in her abilities and she underestimated mine. Her assistant, Ronna Uruburru, was friendly and helpful and Gonterman left her in charge most of the time as she wasn't around much; no one home to guard the henhouse.

The court operations in Long Beach continued much as they had before, but there was one accomplishment in Long Beach that gave me a great deal of satisfaction, and it had nothing to do with the job. I asked my secretary to contact all the judicial assistants (J.A.s) and schedule a meeting with them the next morning at 8:00 a.m. in Department C, the courtroom right across from my office. Because I had previously been a judicial assistant, several of them knew me, but there were others that didn't. Gaining their trust was my first goal. Sure, it's easy to be the boss and bark orders, but that wasn't my style. I led by example. So, during that first meeting where I created a friendly and open atmosphere, I casually asked if there were any unresolved issues that concerned them. One of the J.A.s, Jim Matthews, spoke up and said his courtroom computer was always giving him fits and that the computer staff just couldn't fix the problem. With a room full of J.A.s, I told him point blank the issue would be resolved that day. A few laughs broke the barrier. Jokingly, he said, "Yeah, right." Everyone chuckled. So I prodded him and asked if a bet for a free lunch would interest him. The next day, Jim bought me lunch at my new favorite lunch spot, The Rock Bottom on Ocean Blvd. My computer experience saved me once again (bad NIC) and I gained the respect of several skeptics in the process. But that is not the accomplishment that gave me personal satisfaction. I'll come to that shortly.

To start with, I had an assistant manager in Long Beach who was poison with the employees. She was overbearing and talked down to just about everyone. Although she was usually correct, her interpersonal skills were in need of a doctor. When she made a monumental blunder and insulted one of the judges, I had my opportunity to act. Although she was a close friend of mine, I really had no other choice. Informed there were no managers available to replace her, I asked Jim Matthews if he would like the opportunity to act in her spot, without promotion and on top of his other duties. He was hesitant, yet convincing him wasn't difficult. Where my assistant had been poison, Jim's relationship with the J.A.s was outstanding, respectful and team oriented. He was pleasant, cordial, and he always showed concern for their issues. Those traits smoothed the waters and left me time to pursue other interests: the judges.

Over the next few couple months I had a number opportunities to interface with the judiciary and made several friends, two in particular, Gary Ferrari and Arthur Jean. Gary and Art were walk-a-hol-ics and walked home from the courthouse nearly every day, a distance of more than 5 miles. Shortly thereafter, I was part of that group and enjoyed the discussions and interactions with them and others. There simply aren't enough good adjectives in the English language to describe Gary and Art. Sure, they were both well-educated and very astute in their profession, but more than that, they were just plain good guys, friendly, witty, funny and loyal. It was an absolute pleasure working with them.

Court unification was in process and each district was instructed to prepare a unification plan incorporating all the employees from both court jurisdictions. The municipal court administrators and the superior court administrators each prepared a plan for their courts. Gonterman prepared her plan and I prepared mine. One item on mine caught everyone's attention, especially downtown. Where Sharon drew her plan and showed me as her assistant, I completely left her off of mine. When she confronted me and told me I was moving too fast, I just told her to take a Valium. When she asked me why I had left her off the plan, I told her she wasn't going to be there. Actually, I told Ronna who had been asked by Sharon to inquire. As usual, Sharon was nowhere to be seen. In the end she wasn't. When court unification finally arrived, there was only one administrator from the municipal courts appointed to run a district. It was Ronna, Gonterman's assistant, and the reason she was appointed was because Mr. Clarke had asked me point blank if I thought she could handle the position. I could have sunk her right there, but I didn't. I told Mr. Clarke that I believed Ronna could do as good a job as anyone he had in mind. It was a fair and honest assessment, as well as deserved.

There were plenty of reasons why Gonterman failed, but the one point that solidified my position in Long Beach is that through example and open discussions, I exposed her weaknesses and her self-serving attitude. There were a great deal of differences between case tracking and case management and Sharon had absolutely no idea what they were.

Getting back to my personal accomplishment in Long Beach, I had taken the time and effort to speak to all the employees as I had in the past. Jim Matthews was my accomplishment and I'll explain why. He had passed the promotional exam, but finding a spot for him was difficult.

He had been openly bad-mouthed by Zoe Venhuizen, another district administrator who had mentioned to others that she would never think of promoting him. Zoe was incredibly bright to be sure, but as a manager, she was insensitive to her staff, and she was almost demoted for screwing up the West District a few years before. Her problem was she was her own biggest fan. Now, you may wonder why I didn't promote Jim in Long Beach. Well, I couldn't. I had been given another assignment and was no longer the administrator in Long Beach. I had been reassigned to the darkest court in the county, the Compton Courthouse.

Thankfully, I had a trick up my sleeve. My wife, Carol, was a manager in the Central District in downtown Los Angeles. She had an open spot and Jim moved into court management. His presence in Carol's operation was congruent to his presence in mine as Jim's calm demeanor and relationship with the J.A.s eased a difficult time for Carol downtown. Jim Matthews had been given an opportunity and he seized it, but more than that he did so with dignity and loyalty. One of the J.A.s in Long Beach called me one day and said, "Thank you for giving Jim Matthews a chance." It was a nice gesture, but wasn't really needed. Jim earned his chance. Nothing was given to him.

That should be a lesson for you two. No matter how smart or how much of a genius you may be, if you cannot interact with others with courtesy and respect, you'll spend your career continually dodging obstacles. Give others the opportunity and they'll clear the obstacles for you.

Chapter 42: The South Central District (Compton)

Well, it was here. The year "2000" (or Y2K as it was called) finally emerged on the scene. Mandated court unification was now happening. I was looking forward to the many improvements needed in Long Beach when Gary Ferrari called me to his chambers just before lunch. Art Jean was already there as was John Clarke. Mr. Clarke asked me straightforwardly if I would take another assignment, one that was fraught with uncertainty. I just smiled and said, "Put me where I'm needed." On Monday, January 3, 2000, I would be assigned as the District Administrator in the South Central District of the Los Angeles Superior Court. I would be in Compton.

My assignment to Compton was the most daunting, most challenging, and absolutely the most rewarding assignment of my career. It was also my last.

Career moves are ever-changing and this was certainly no exception. Just the week before, I had paid a visit to Jim Manczarek, the Court Manager in Compton for the Superior Court, for a tour of the facility. Of the many managers I have known in the court, I had always respected Jim for his brevity, wit, and calm demeanor. He was one of the good guys and he was incredibly intelligent. His brother, Ray, was keyboard player for some rock band called "the Doors" with some lead singer named Jim Morrison.

On our tour of the facility, he showed me the parking area under the courthouse and I asked him where his parking spot was since I would be coming to Compton the following week. It was buried somewhere in the

171

vast canyon of cars and he said it was spot #148 or something like that. When nearing the entrance of the courthouse, I noticed a shiny red sports car adjacent to the entry. On the wall above that shiny red sports car were the words "Municipal Court Administrator." Jim informed me that was Tim Aguilar's parking space.

On my arrival the morning of January 3, 2000, I drove into the parking structure and promptly parked near the entrance to the courthouse under a sign that read "Municipal Court Administrator" and was immediately approached by a Deputy Sheriff who told me that was Mr. Aguilar's parking space. Since there was no longer a Municipal Court Administrator as there was no longer a municipal court, I said, "When Mr. Aguilar arrives, tell him to park in spot #148." It was my first day in Compton and I had just slammed the most powerful and influential municipal court administrator in the county. That shockwave went countywide at the speed of lightning. That was the easy part, the hard part was just around the corner.

I spent the first week mingling with the staff and quietly observing the operations in a warm and free-spirited manner. As I had always done, I spoke to each and every employee of both courts individually, and what I learned disturbed me. The previous superior court clerical staff was in disarray and mistrust was so thick you could slice it. The scenario in the previous municipal court was even worse. Employees in both courts were scared and uncertain of their jobs as the merger of the municipal and superior courts was forced on them. Not just that, but the working conditions were like night and day in the two courts. The superior court clerical office facilities looked like a cheap motel. The municipal court facilities looked like the Ritz-Carlton. Two completely different worlds separated by arrogance, mistrust, and the mistaken belief each was better than the other. They were different to be sure, but better?

On a more pleasant note, I enjoyed interacting with the judiciary from both previous courts. It was one judiciary now, but the old lines would take a while to blend together. Collectively, the 32 judicial officers in the South Central District were some of the warmest, friendliest, and most sincere that I ever had the opportunity to work with in any capacity. Without exception, they were all deeply concerned with the surrounding community and they participated any way they could to make it better.

The most blatant observation I found in Compton was that there was no competition between the judges. Never before had I encountered such behavior, but then again, I had never met a judge like John Cheroske. "Judge C" as I referred to him, was a leader, the leader. He knew what needed to be done and no problem getting his way. I'll get this out of the way now in case I forget later. John Cheroske was the best judicial officer I ever encountered and my respect for that man is unwavering.

After I had spoken with all the employees, I had my secretary set up a meeting for 8:00 a.m. in the Jury Assembly Room with all the employees of the previous two court operations who not only didn't speak to each other, they didn't seem to care for each other either. I had learned a great deal about them; they were now going to learn about me.

With approximately 250 or so employees present, I greeted them and opened, "Whatever has happened to you in the past that was distasteful, mean-spirited or you believe has negatively affected your career is gone. None of it matters to me. What does matter is fairness and giving everyone an equal opportunity to excel. Before I go any further, I want all of you to stand up and change places. Sit beside someone you don't know and introduce yourselves to them." I was about to make the breakthrough I was hoping for when I asked, "How many of you from the former municipal court are on a promotional list?" Not a single hand went up. It was also a question where I already knew the answer. So I asked again. Same response. When I inquired why, someone finally spoke up and said it was useless to take promotional exams because all the promotions in the municipal court were made because of nepotism.

One after another agreed and said if you weren't on good terms with the managers, you wouldn't and didn't get promoted. Tim Aguilar sat silently in the front row and never turned his head. "Not anymore," I told them. I explained to them that from now on, the ones scoring the highest on the exams would be selected for any open positions. "If you do your job well, assist others when the opportunity arises, and pay attention through observation, you should do well on the exams. Not only that, but your supervisors will take notice," I assured them. It took several months before the trend turned my way, but the clerical staff opened up and grew to appreciate each other and openly assist one another whenever and wherever they could.

Merging the operations of two separate, but in many ways congruent, court operations wasn't as difficult as some might believe. The one stumbling block was the budget, as always seemed to be the case. The superior court had always run budget operations from a central location, in downtown Los Angeles. The municipal courts were each operated autonomously and because of that, they received funding from many sources and not just from the county. Because I had come from the previous superior court, I clearly saw the opportunities to move in a constructive direction and did. Within a year, the Compton Courthouse clerical operations were completely remodeled and the facilities were dazzling. No longer were there two separate environments.

Tim Aguilar, the previous administrator, was on his way out the door and he knew it. He and I spoke candidly at lunch one day where he told me John Clarke was going to get rid of him. I already knew that, but said nothing to Tim. What I will say here is that Tim Aguilar was different from the other municipal court administrators I had to usurp. Where Chris Crawford and Sharon Gonterman had been legends in their own mind, Tim Aguilar was a visionary and a very smart individual. He may have done things that superior court management didn't like and he may not have acted professionally at times, and he certainly didn't nurture his staff very well, but he was brilliant. He implemented concepts that were beneficial to his community, to the court, and to the County of Los Angeles. Were he and I close friends? No. Did I like him as a person? Yes, I did.

DAILY JOURNAL EXTRA **LITIGATION FILES** AUGUST 19, 2002 7

Court Administrator Teaches Jurors a Lesson
Prospective Panelists Hear Highlights of American Legal System

By Jeffrey Anderson

Aside from free coffee and the efficient chill of central air conditioning, there at first seems to be nothing uplifting about being in the jury room of the Compton Courthouse at 8 a.m. on this sweltering Monday morning.

"How many of you are proud to be here today?" Steve Forest, administrator of the court says, inviting a tentative show of hands from less than half of the 250 Los Angeles County residents in attendance.

Forest stands jacketless at a podium, his back straight as an arrow, a microphone clipped neatly to his tie.

His shoulders swivel along with his head as he surveys the room. A half-smile is fixed on his face.

"How many of you are proud to be Americans?" he says, this time drawing a nearly unanimous response.

"I wonder what accounts for the difference?" Forest says softly, almost as if he's talking to himself.

On the wall behind him is a homemade sign that reads "Jury Assembly Room," with a smiley face and the word "Smile" below it. A Subway sandwich poster invites the public to "Ask the jury office for savings coupons."

Across the room, a cabinet full of puzzles is stationed near the soda machine and the Sparklets water cooler.

Just to Forest's right is a home-theater sized TV, which is waiting to entertain citizens who will sit here until their names are

Photo by Hugh Williams

Steve Forest delights in the devout patriotism of Virginia statesman George Mason who protested the lack of civil rights provisions in the original draft of the Constitution.

When he gets to the American Revolution, Forest offers detailed accounts of the colonial revolt against the British Army following the Stamp Act, which temporarily vanquished the right to trial by jury.

called to jury rooms in one of the county's 58 courthouses, according to the public information office of the Los Angeles County Superior Court.

If the options available on the automat-

Briefly

Silver

Judge Richard Silver, 60, joined the San Jose office of JAMS, a private alternative dispute resolution provider, as a resolution expert late last month. Although he's officially part of the San Jose office, Silver will work throughout Monterey County.

Silver served on the Monterey Superior Court from 1977 to 2002. Before that, he was a litigation partner at Heisler, Stewart, Silver & Daniels in Carmel.

■ ■ ■ ■

Clare Gibson took over the reins as Larkspur city attorney recently. Gibson, an associate at San Leandro's Meyers, Nave, Riback, Silver & Wilson, previously served as assistant city attorney under Richard Rudnansky, who is a partner at Meyers Nave. Larkspur has used Meyers Nave for its city attorney work for the past four years.

■ ■ ■ ■

The American Inns of Court has moved into the age of technology. Beginning in July, the organization is providing training on the Internet through West LegalEdcenter at www.westlegaledcenter.com. American Inns of Court provides continuing

Jury Orientation

Supreme Court of California

350 McALLISTER STREET
SAN FRANCISCO, CA 94102-4783

August 20, 2002

CARLOS R. MORENO
ASSOCIATE JUSTICE

Mr. Steve Forest
District Court Administrator
Los Angeles Superior Court
200 West Compton Boulevard
Compton, CA 90220

Dear Mr. Forest:

    I wish to commend you for your outstanding juror orientation presentation which was featured in the *Daily Journal* on August 19, 2002. As a former judge of the Compton Municipal Court from 1986 to 1993 I made the same presentation to hundreds of jurors in the same assembly room in the Compton Courthouse, although not as eloquently as you are doing. As a federal judge, administering the oath of citizenship to new citizens, I reminded them of their many obligations as new citizens, among them the obligation to serve as trial jurors in our courts.

    Thank you for your excellent service and dedication to our jury system.

                Very truly yours,

                CARLOS R. MORENO

CRM:pcs

176

Chapter 43: Closing My Career

Over the years, in my opinion, I had accomplished a great deal, assisted many with their careers, and had my head on the line more times than I can recall. But as my assignment to Compton was eventually the undoing to my career, it was also of my own doing and my own choice, and I would have done nothing different if I had the opportunity to do it over.

With court unification complete (in name only), there was now time to relax a bit and pursue those little things that bring a smile to your face. In the Compton facility, I had a number of employees who were passed over for promotion for any number of reasons, and I'm sure those who passed them over had their reasons. They just weren't my reasons. Stan Ferrell, Mona McClure, and Rene Casares from the previous superior court come to mind. I had known all of them previously, but now I was in a position where I could, and did, make a difference in their lives.

There wasn't much I could do for the managers from the previous municipal court as Tim Aguilar pulled a fantastico that enraged superior court management downtown. Just prior to court unification, Mr. Aguilar promoted all his managers up one level and there was nothing that could be done to unwrap that situation. I have to hand it to Tim; I probably would have done the same thing in his position. Good for them.

During my first year in Compton, I had the pleasure of promoting more than 40 individuals to higher level positions and I did so gladly. Not only that, but I promoted individuals from other courts who chose to come and work in Compton. Within a year, the South Central District (Compton Court) was the pinnacle of success in Los Angeles County. But my task was not nearly finished.

Stan Ferrell was a judicial assistant who had tried for years to promote into management, yet was continually denied. When the promotional exam for managers was posted, I asked Stan if he was taking the exam. He said no. He told me he was finished with exams and the disappointment that followed, but the tide was changing for him. I told him point blank, "Stan. If you take the exam and pass it, I'll promote you. Period. End of story." What could he say as he had witnessed first-hand the promotions coming out of the Compton Court. When I told the employees I would do something, it was done. Not once in my entire career did I waver or back away from a promise and I wasn't going to start now. You see, I had known the same disappointment as Stan and managed to get past it by performance and luck. Fortunately, I had someone who cleared the way for me to move into management. A little guardian angel never hurt anyone and so I told Stan.

Mona McClure held the highest clerical position in the office and she had an extremely beneficial relationship with the surrounding community. She, too, had been slammed and misused by previous managers. There were a number of occasions where I had the opportunity to use Mona's insight and contacts. The one that comes to mind involves Carol's daughter, Lisa.

She worked for a publishing company that was looking to donate 10,000 books for a tax write-off. When I discussed the donation with Lisa, she said her boss wanted to donate 10,000 classic novels to a school or civic organization. Lisa arranged for me to meet with her boss and I brought Mona with me. What transpired was a community gathering where those 10,000 classic novels were donated to Compton High School, thanks to Mona. The gathering was attended by Yvonne Braithwaite Burke, one of the 5 supervisors in Los Angeles County, Jessie Jackson (always looking for a way to get free publicity), the mayor of Compton, many of the Compton High School student body and teachers, and several of our judicial officers. How Jessie Jackson learned of the event is a mystery. It was also televised over the local television channel. It was a resounding success that benefitted the publisher, the schools, Mona McClure and the superior court. A bonding relationship between the community and the courts had been born that day and, hopefully, continues.

Rene Casares was a judicial assistant also trying to move up the ladder; unfortunately, he suffered from bad publicity. Rene was a fairly good judicial assistant; he was genuine and everyone knew it. More than that, he was loyal and hard working. He oozed confidence and was always willing to take on any assignment, no matter the difficulty. There were three judicial assistants taking a promotional exam for Senior Judicial Assistant and I called them to my office during lunch one day and told them that each was highly qualified in my eyes and that to make sure there were no games being played or backroom deals being offered, I told all three that whomever scored the highest on the exam got the spot. In a close contest, Rene was the guy who made the top score of the three.

Stan, Mona and Rene are three success stories that garnish my memories of working for the superior court. There were many others, of course, but these three stand out in my mind for the simple reason they pulled themselves up when given the "opportunity" to do so. I can't remember a time that I did not see smiles on their faces or a brisk step in their walk. They were proud of their accomplishments and they should have been.

All of my successes within the Compton Court didn't exactly hold good feelings with management downtown, especially John Clarke. The issue that caused them the greatest amount of discomfort was the collections division I had that was instituted by Tim Aguilar. As I mentioned earlier, Tim was a visionary and he instituted a collection division in the Compton Municipal Court that employed 10 individuals. With a small staff, the collections division in Compton collected 35% of all the collections money revenue in the entire state, and yet I was instructed to dismember the operation.

On examination, there was no real justification to do so. Just because it was instituted by Tim Aguilar, management wanted it gone. However, on closer inspection, something appeared definitely wrong. With the collections division gone, all the collections accounts would be handed over to a private company: GC Services. Perhaps that wasn't a bad thing until I discovered that on GC Services payroll, overseeing collections for the court, was a gentleman by the name of Ed Kritzman who just happened to be the previous Executive Officer of the Los Angeles Superior Court. Was there collusion or other self-serving interests somewhere lurking in the background. No one will ever know, but I'm sure that in today's economic climate, a different scenario would have proved much more beneficial for the court.

With the backing and support of the judiciary in Compton, I struggled unsuccessfully to keep the collections division open. Support also flowed in from the local communities that would benefit from keeping collections in Compton. It didn't matter and in the end, it ended my career. When the opportunity came for John Clarke to end it, he did. Can't say I that I blame him either. Did I have any hard feelings about it? Nope! There weren't any as I had made an earlier decision that if I did not prevail, I would just walk away. As the situation as I saw it unfolded, I stood my ground and did what I believed was right, and I'd do it exactly the same way again. I was not successful and because of my defiant stance against court management, my career with the court was finished. I just walked away, but with my head held high. I was incredibly fortunate to have worked in a career that was truly intoxicating at times, difficult in others, but absolutely the best thing I could have done.

Chapter 44: What Now ? ? ?

Well, my working career was over and that chapter in my life had closed. Just as I had closed previous chapters, I didn't look back. I was still a Buscaglia disciple and everything I had learned from him had a positive feel to it so I went forward trusting in the belief that life was a good thing to be enjoyed to its fullest. I have mentioned Leo Buscaglia many times throughout my story, but I have had other heroes and I'll mention them now while I can still recall.

My personal heroes:
John Adams
Richard Henry Lee
George Mason
Abraham Lincoln
Russell H. Conwell
Felice Leonardo Buscaglia
Ricardo Torres
Johnny Johnson
John Cheroske

Not a long list, I know, but a truly respectful one. You'll recognize all the names on the list, save one: Johnny Johnson.

Johnny Johnson was the Assistant Executive Office during the time that Jim Dempsey was the Executive Officer of the Superior Court prior to court unification. I'm not entirely sure, but I believe he later became the CEO in Ojai, California. In any event, Johnny was a mentor to me in my career with the court and he did so with open honesty, warmth, and always with a smile. He seemed to recognize the fire in me and put it to good use for the superior court. I warmly mention him here simply because of all of the people I reported to in management, he is the only one I truly respected. Don't take this the wrong way, I sincerely respected the positions that others held above me, but that doesn't mean I respected the person. Johnny Johnson is the one person I encountered in my entire career who had no hidden agenda. He was the real deal. If he openly helped you or mentored you, it was because he wanted to and for no other reason.

About six months after I retired, Carol and I moved from crowded California to Lewis County, Washington, where we built a house and began a relaxing way of life that felt refreshing. The sky was clear and clean and it took a while to get used to the fact that I couldn't see what I was breathing. Life was a lot slower and a traffic jam amounted to three cars in a row going in the same direction. Beauty was everywhere and we were completely surrounded by the absence of stress. Our new home found us entrenched in the southern part of the Cascades in southwestern Washington state overlooking Lake Mayfield. Our closest neighbors were elk, deer, chipmunks, porcupines, eagles and those little black and white smelly creatures.

The year was 2004 and since I had always been athletic, I found peace and joy in running and hiking, and I discovered that smelling the roses wasn't as difficult as I thought. The area was stunningly beautiful as well as peaceful. It took me at least 5 minutes to get used to the idea of being retired. I haven't kept in close contact with many of the folks in California, except Gary and Art and a few others. Those folks down there are still struggling through life while I am here climbing trees, hiking the mountains, and fishing for Gus.

Oh, Gus. He's the little 5 pound brown trout that I have hooked and lost several times. Actually, I let him go a few times. Besides trout, there are two types of salmon, Tiger Muskie, and bass available in the lake. The Cowlitz River is loaded with fish, frogs and other creatures and the mountains are packed with all sorts of critters. It's the best place to be.

Chapter 45: The Accident

Sunday morning, February 26, 2006.

There had been a fierce winter wind storm in January and it downed at least a dozen trees on our property. Carol was at church so I decided to do a little cutting and provide free firewood to our neighbors. My dog, Shade, leaped into the back of my Jeep and down Tanglewood we rode, making a hard right onto Sugar Pine and then up the hill.

After a short survey session, I got out the small Skil chainsaw and went to work, cutting two large maples into small-size chunks, about 15" in length. The circles were about 3' across, so splitting them later would be an easy task. After about an hour, a new white Hummer pulled up. It was Darrell Benson, one of our neighbors, who asked me if I wanted to sell my lot on Deer Park (love that name). We chatted for a few minutes and he left without the answer he wanted.

Further down Sugar Pine were several more downed trees, mostly alders which were much easier to disassemble and the logs would burn hot. After I had cut perhaps 4 or 5 trees into 15"-18" chunks, I decided I was just about done, but still had one tough alder to deal with so I hiked over to it. It was down, like the others, but not completely. The roots were still in the ground. I stood to the right side and began to cut. With all the tension still in the 80' tree, I knew after it was cut that the remaining "stump" would spring back to its natural position.

As the blade was cutting through the tree, I thought to myself, "This is going easy . . ." It happened faster than lightning and I didn't feel a thing. Instead of moving back to its original position, the tree sprung sideways catching me under my left leg. I looked up as the tree was going down and noticed blood. I looked down at my Levis. The bone from my left femur had torn through my pants and was sticking through about 6 inches; blood was spurting out in rhythmic streams. I was in deep trouble and knew it immediately. I stood up on my good leg and said, "Is that all you've got?" Still defiant after all these years.

I mentioned at the beginning of incredible coincidence and personal circumstance. Two things happened that kept me alive. First was personal circumstance: my physical conditioning program. I was 60 years old and in incredible physical condition. Over the years I had been a bike rider, water & snow skier, basketball player, avid golfer, distance runner and power walker. I loved competing in just about any sport. In California, before we moved to Washington, I would walk (speed or power walk) 40 to 50 miles a week, going up and down the hills surrounding Signal Hill in Long Beach with a couple of good friends, Art Jean and Gary Ferrari. Art and Gary were Superior Court Judges and we had been to Europe with them twice. On the first trip, I climbed Mt. Etna in Sicily. Art and Gary were to climb it with me, but silly reasons didn't allow them to do it. Additionally, I had participated in my first Long Beach Marathon at age 55 and finished 4th in my age bracket. Not bad for an old fart. When we first moved to Washington in January of 2004, I would jog (in the snow) down to Highway 12 and back, a distance of 7½ miles. I hiked everywhere and just couldn't get enough of the beauty and serenity of the mountains.

After the tree had taken me down, I did something without thinking. I took off my belt and made a tourniquet above the wound in my leg, slowing the bleeding and quite possibly saving my own life. I still had no pain and called Shade to my side. He was barking. I said, "Shade, let's sit here a minute and maybe take a little nap." I couldn't move and I was bleeding badly, the blood warm against the cool air. I felt it was probably over, the end of the line, and I was calm and at peace without fear of death so I thought I'd just talk to my dog. The second part of this miracle was already in motion.

Three lady friends who took almost daily walks around the mountains had stopped by earlier and asked if I wanted to join them. I politely declined as I was focused on the stupid job I was doing. On their way back up the hill, they didn't follow their usual route. Instead and for reasons unknown, they were walking on my property when the tree went down and they came by to investigate and saw Shade barking. Now for the good part. Two of the ladies were nurses, one (Meem Davenport) worked in the E.R. at Emmanuel Hospital in Portland. The other nurse, Linda Brock, called 911 to activate Life Flight (helicopter no less). Then she called Kelly Morrison who is a friend and EMT for the Fire Department. Within minutes the place was swarming with activity. I remember being pulled up out of the hole I was in and placed on a gurney. The Paramedics drove me down to the Lake Mayfield Youth Camp where the helicopter would meet us. I remember Meem saying to me, "You're never alone when you have friends, Steve."

I was still conscious when I was given a shot that put me to sleep. The chopper was going to take me to Seattle, but it was a longer flight than Portland and the weather was bad. Enter my friend, Meem, who was the E.R. nurse. She demanded I be taken to the trauma ward at Emmanuel Hospital in Portland, a shorter flight. Off I went and in 30 minutes I was wheeled into surgery.

Carol was on her way home from church when she was notified of my accident. She saw me in the chopper just before I left. I was blue. Tom and June Wente, two neighbor friends, drove her to Portland in just over an hour (90 mile drive). On arriving, Carol was told that a doctor wanted to talk to her in a private room which was not a good sign. He told her that I was still alive, but he didn't know why. I shouldn't have been. The human body contains about 24 units of blood. I had lost 22.

When I awoke from an induced coma 10 days later, I was a mess. I was bloated like a frog and had tubes everywhere: 3 in my side, four in my mouth, and two in my nose. I couldn't talk, couldn't move. It would be more than a month before I could write a single letter on a tablet. I had no control of any of my muscles and that feeling left me with a sense of pitiful helplessness. My left leg was three times its normal size. I was soon to learn the extent of my injuries and they were many.

Injuries:
1. broken left ankle;
2. triple break of the left tibia;
3. compound fracture to the left femur;
4. sciatic nerve severed behind left thigh (hence no pain);
5. femoral artery severed;
6. broken pelvis;
7. broken sternum
8. left side of chest caved in (ribs broken)
9. punctured left lung;
10. gash on left arm (that was the one that bugged me most)

I underwent several surgeries the first day. One to stop the bleeding. The vascular surgeon removed about 6 inches of a vein form my right leg and "spliced" it to the torn femoral artery in my left. The neurosurgeon stitched the sciatic nerves back together as best he could. Then came the real tricky part. My left knee was shattered and unrecognizable. It wasn't there. Looked like the Milky Way in the x-rays. Surgery after surgery would slowly mend my broken body and I endured a total of 30 surgeries over the next several months before I was 'almost' healed.

Slowly I climbed back into life. For weeks I laid motionless, unable to communicate. A nurse came in one morning and said they would be removing my tubes today. Yeah! I wanted to drink something! When the intern came in he lifted my robe and said, "This might hurt." What was he doing? He braced himself and then pulled two tubes out of my left side that had provided assistance to my punctured left lung. The tubes in my mouth remained and still I could not speak. I was still trapped. This was horrible and yet I stubbornly endured.

One morning my 11-year old daughter, Alicia, appeared in the doorway looking very solemn. She didn't say a word. Without hesitation, she walked over to the side of my bed, turned and faced the door while placing her hand on my shoulder. She then stood at attention as if she were a guard. She was. She was my guard. My darling little girl had taken command and was not about to let any more harm come to her dad. The essay she wrote in the beginning of this story came from that experience and she must have been deeply distressed. You may be only one person in the world, but you may also be the world to one person.

One of my orthopedic surgeons, a very attractive young lady name Tamara (can't remember her last name) paid me the ultimate compliment. She was the first orthopedic surgeon to work on my leg as she was on E.R. duty that day, and told Carol that she thought I was a much younger man until she saw the salt & pepper hair. Must admit, my legs had been finely tuned from my rigorous life style, but now things were far different. An interesting note on Tamara is that her favorite past time was barrel-horse riding at rodeos, and she was an orthopedic doctor no less.

My leg was a mess and terribly swollen. I went into surgery several times to have the wounds cleaned and repaired. When the time was right my leg was placed into an Ilizarov. The device is a specialized form of external fixator, a circular fixator, modular in construction. Stainless steel rings are fixed to the bone via stainless heavy-gauge wire (called "pins"). The rings are connected to each other with threaded rods attached through adjustable nuts. The circular construction and tensioned wires of the Ilizarov apparatus provide far more structural support than the traditional monolateral fixator system. This allows early weight-bearing. The frame can be used to support a fractured limb, but it is most commonly used to correct deformity through distraction osteogenesis.

I had 28 "pins" that went through my leg (and bones) and attached to the Ilizarov rings. I have long legs and the surgeon, Dr. Richard Gellman, said it was the longest one he had constructed for a patient. Yeah, and about 35-40 pounds of metal, too. The pins were there to reposition my broken bones in correct alignment to the knee. Dr. Gellman said I would have the device on anywhere from 16 to 24 months, and it would be at least 2 years before I could walk again. He told me that any walking I could do would strengthen the bones. So the more I could walk (walker or crutches) the faster I would heal. He had no idea how that would motivate me. Before surgery, he would come in and talk with me, always inquiring if I had any questions. I always said no. I told him it would be okay or it wouldn't, and that I always had complete trust and faith in him. He always smiled when leaving.

Nearly two months into my hospital stay I decided I needed a haircut. My hair was continually wet, then dry and matted, then wet again from all the medication, chills and sweats, etc. I needed a break. Around 2:00 a.m. one morning, a male nurse came by to check on me and I asked if he had access to clippers. He said he didn't, but there may be some in the O/R. He returned a few minutes later with barber shears and asked if I would like a trim. "Buzz it all off," was my request. There! No more matted hair and I actually felt refreshed. I liked the way it felt. It was a comfortable feeling, too. Been buzzing ever since. Guess I'm just lazy.

My stay in the hospital lasted 75 days. When I was discharged, the nurses had a party for me. Due to my goofy demeanor, they genuinely seemed to like my silly antics, practical jokes and positive nature. Denise, the head nurse, made a statement that touched me dearly. She said, "Mr. Forrest . . ." I interrupted her and said, "Call me Steve." She said, "Okay, Mr. Forrest, you have been here at Emmanuel for 75 days and in all that time, you have had contact with just about all of my staff—AND—you have not complained about anything. Not once." And they all started clapping. Wow! Nice send off.

A hospital bed was waiting when I returned home in mid-May. Shade was happy to see me and there were lots of visitors, although I was weak and didn't really want any. I put on a good show, but didn't want any sympathy. That word is not in my vocabulary. With nothing to do except watch television, I laid there flat on my back until the end of July when a physical therapist arrived and got me out of bed. With a great deal of encouragement, I was able to stand and take 2 steps with a walker. My left calf muscles had atrophied and my leg looked like a toothpick with bullet holes, canyons, racing stripes and a couple divots thrown in for good measure. Just 2 steps and I was out of breath, completely exhausted. It must have taken a couple minutes just to accomplish that one simple task, but it was a start I thought. He said that next week the goal was 6 steps (to the door). I responded, "Nope. We're going out to the deck."

That's exactly what happened as I made it outside and sat huffing, puffing and sweating for several minutes before heading back inside. Over the next few months I grew stronger and started using the walker more and more. I would do laps around the deck and driveway which is more than

200 feet long, and I was building callouses on both hands from all the walking. The same regimen happened when I started with crutches. By December, a little more than 8 months from the time the Ilizarov was placed on my leg, it came off. Not the 16-24 months the doctor had said. On February 26, 2007, I took my first steps unassisted by any device. One year to the day and I was walking.

My physical therapist, Holly Gullickson, was another character I had to deal with. She was a master at her profession with a personality that matched so I nick-named her "the pain-master" for her ability to cause discomfort with just one finger. My leg had been in a horizontal position, locked in place, for 9 months and could not bend because of the scar tissue and calcification of the torn cartilage. After healing, my leg would bend about 20 degrees at the knee and that was it. The knee had been shattered and was full of calcified cartilage and scar tissue. Holly explained that all the benefits of physical therapy would be accomplished the first 12 weeks. After that everything remains status-quo. After 12 weeks, I managed to get to 40 degrees or so, but not much more. She said any further gain was unlikely. She didn't know me very well, but another nightmare was on the way that I had to conquer.

During one of my P.T. sessions, mucous started oozing from the skin graft on my left leg. Holly was concerned and told me to mention it to the doctor when I saw him next. My follow-up appointment with Dr. Gellman was set the following week, but was moved up when I called about the problem. On examination, Dr. Gellman had me admitted to Emmanuel Hospital that day. After tests were run, Dr. Gellman told Carol that a serious infection had set in and it was probably time to remove the leg, just above the knee. He told her not to say anything to me as he wanted to do it and she reluctantly agreed. That afternoon, Dr. Gellman broke the news to me and said he would have specialists come see me about a prosthetic device and that his partner, Dr. Dean Beaman would be in to see me in the morning. They did, but I paid little attention to what was said and thanked them for their time without making a decision.

Dr. Beaman arrived bright and early the next morning and I greeted him with a broad smile. On seeing him I said, "Hi, doc, what brings you here?" Along with his P.A. (Physician's Assistant), he reiterated what Dr. Gellman had stated the previous afternoon. He said the infection was probably caused because of a medication I didn't receive, although I should have. He proceeded to write the 5 problems I had with my leg on a whiteboard and explained each one as he wrote. When he concluded he asked what I thought. I said, "Do you want an honest answer?" He nodded.

I told him to cross-off the word 'problem' and I waited until he did. "Now, write the word 'challenge' above it because I will never, ever give up." A wry grin crossed his face and I continued, "Looks like I have 2 options. First, I can try to conquer this infection and save my sanity. Second, you can chop off my leg. If I go for #2, I can't do #1 and that, my friend, is not acceptable." He looked over to his P.A. and they both chuckled.

He explained what I would have to do in order to achieve my goal. "You'll be sent home for two weeks until the infection is cleared and you cannot put any pressure on your leg. The rod has been removed and any pressure on your left leg will cause it to break. If that happens, there is no choice." Okay! In order to go through the process, I went into surgery again to have a 'pick line' embedded in my chest so that the medication I would receive could be injected directly into my heart three times daily.

Obviously, as you guys know, I made it through that ordeal and had a new and different type of rod placed in my leg. I would remain on medication for 6 months with follow-up appointments every couple weeks. I had made it past the point of no return and was on the mend, for good this time.

Back in P.T. (Physical therapy), Holly kept pushing and pulling and I kept telling her she was a wimp. She laughed and caused more discomfort. I was now up to 60 degrees of flexibility. She told me it made no sense that I should continue to improve. I just told her I wasn't ready to quit.

On my next, and last, visit to Dr. Gellman, he told me there was nothing further he could do for me. Although my leg had been reconstructed, it was still stiff and with only 60 degrees of flexibility, I asked to be referred to a knee specialist. He agreed and referred me to his friend, Dr. Scott Grewe in Portland. His office made the referral and appointment for me.

On meeting Dr. Grewe for the first time, we shook hands and I told him, "Richard Gellman said you're the finest knee specialist around." He replied, "He better. I operated on his knee." Dr. Grewe and I hit it off right away. After examination, he set me up to have my knee scoped. Afterward, I had slightly more flexibility, but not what I wanted. Dr. Grewe said I was about at the limit, but he would consider a knee replacement only if I could somehow manage 80 degrees of flexibility. I was at 65. "I doubt you can get that much flexibility and a knee replacement at less range of motion than that would be a waste of time.

On my next visit to Holly, I told her I had a new goal. I would shoot for 80 degrees (didn't tell her what Dr. Grewe had said) and she shook her head and said I was a head-case. I was nonchalant about it and said, "We'll see." "No way," she said. Two months later she pushed and stretched my leg and measured it as always before I left: 82 degrees. I called Dr. Grewe for an appointment. During our discussion he described my options, but said the only way to gain a greater range of motion would be a knee replacement. I told him I was a "go for it" guy and knee replacement surgery was scheduled for January 16, 2009.

Just before I went under, Dr. Grewe told me the surgery was routine and all the measurements would be done by computer. I asked if the tibia malunion would be corrected and he said it would. He also said that patients don't trust the surgery initially and are reticent to put weight on the knee. He said the new knee would be stronger than the original and would hold up immediately after surgery.

The surgery went well and I awoke in recovery a few hours later. When the attending nurse asked me how I felt and if I wanted anything, I looked at her and said, "Let's go for a walk." And we did. I had climbed the mountain. After another month of P.T., Holly said, "You're fired. I can do nothing more for you that you can't do yourself. You should be very proud of your accomplishments; I am." And so was I as I was now at 88 degrees (90 degrees and you can sit comfortably at a table). I joined the gym adjacent to Holly's office and kept working.

One morning a few months later I was sitting on the stationary bike stretching my leg when Holly walked by and said, "Why don't you go all the way around." I made a mistake by telling her I couldn't and she said, "What! Are you kidding me? You have never said 'I can't' before." That's all it took. She told me to cheat by lifting my left hip and I tried it. Lots of discomfort, but after a few tries it happened. My leg went completely around, and it hurt. "Takes 110 degrees to ride the bike," she said as she walked away. After a few weeks of work, I was now riding the bike for an hour and without any discomfort.

Well, that's where I am. I have my leg, ugly as it is, and I can walk just fine, although it looks a little different than others. There are times when you can't notice my slight limp at all, others when it bothers me a bit, but it's getting better. Wonderful things can happen with the right attitude and a little luck. Actually, a lot of luck.

Now, I've told quite a story in this final segment, but it's not done. There is just no way I could have done all this without the loving care given to me by my wife, Carol. She was unselfish and always, always there to assist me in my time of need. To be truthful, there was a great deal of need. How can you thank someone who has given you everything . . . you just can't.

I have listed for you a few of my heroes and the impact they have had on my life. Just before I close I want to list a few of the most impressive moments I have encountered in my journey through life:

1. Walking the streets of Pompei . . .
2. Spending 2 days in the Louvre and wanting for more . . .
3. Climbing the Mayan pyramid at Chichen Itza . . .
4. Hiking down to Havazu Falls in the Grand Canyon . . .
5. Climbing Mt Etna in Sicily . . .
6. Scuba diving into the Blue Hole in Belize . . .
7. Parachuting out of an airplane in San Diego . . .
8. Hang-gliding off the coast of California . . .
9. Extreme skiing at Alta, Utah . . . and
10. Being inducted into the U.S. Army on April 21, 1966.

Finally, I will revisit my memories of Leo Buscaglia and relate a story he spoke of regarding an 85-year old man who was near the end of his life when he spoke of how he would lead his life if he had the chance to do it again.

"If I had to live my life over again, I'd make more mistakes next time. I'd relax a lot more. I'd limber up and be sillier than I was on this trip. I know of very few things I would take seriously. I would be crazier and I'd certainly be less hygienic.

I'd take more chances and I'd take more trips and I'd climb more mountains and I'd swim more rivers and I'd watch more sunsets. I'd burn more gasoline and I'd eat more ice cream and less beans. I'd have more actual troubles and fewer imaginary ones. Ninety per-cent of what we worry about never happens anyway.

You see, I was one of those people who lived prophylactically and sanely and sensibly, hour after hour, day after day. Oh, I've had my moments and if I had to do it all over again, I'd have many more of them. In fact, I'd try to have nothing else, just moments, one after the other, instead of living all of my life so many years ahead of myself. I've been one of those people who never went anywhere without a thermometer, a hot water bottle, a gargle, a raincoat and a parachute.

If I had it to do it all over again, I'd travel much more lightly next time. I would start barefoot earlier in the Spring and stay that way later in the Fall and I'd play hookie more and I wouldn't get so many good grades or plan on such a big career except, maybe, as it happened. I'd ride more merry-go-rounds and one thing's for certain—I'd pick more daisies."

Thank you . . .

p.s. I mentioned many times about searching for a lost love. That would be Susan. Well, that's another story, isn't it?